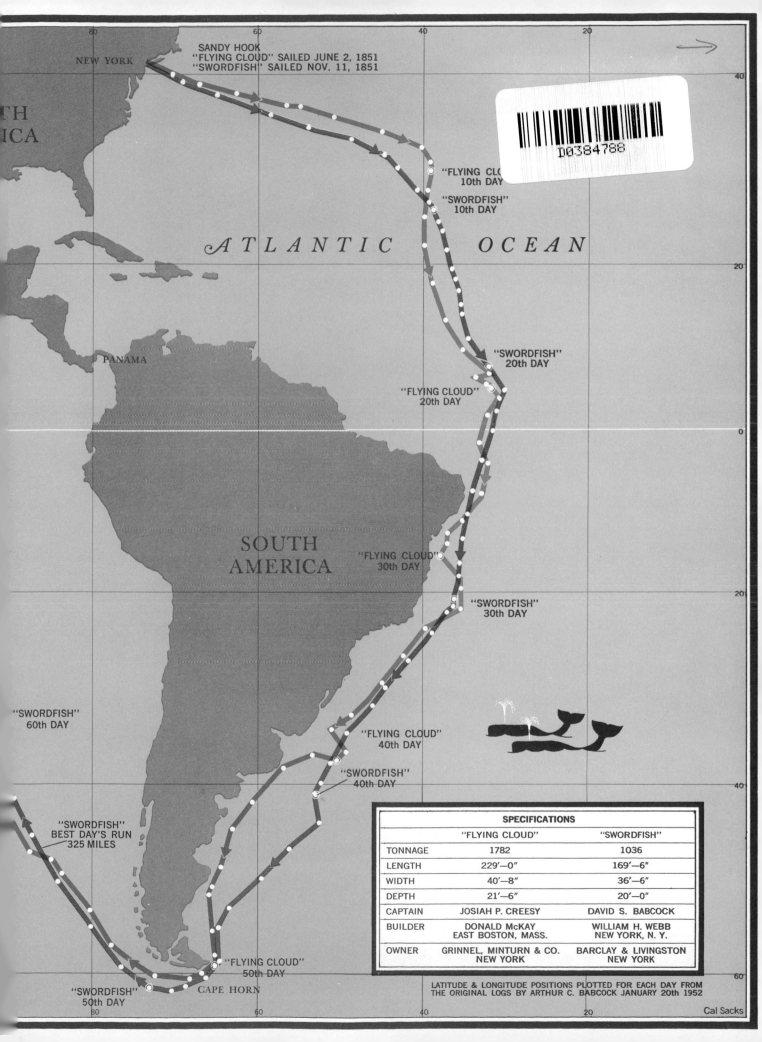

SANDY HOOK
"FLYING CLOUD" SAILED JUNE 2, 1851
"SWORDFISH" SAILED NOV. 11, 1851

NEW YORK

TH
ICA

ATLANTIC   OCEAN

"FLYING CLO
10th DAY

"SWORDFISH"
10th DAY

PANAMA

"SWORDFISH"
20th DAY

"FLYING CLOUD"
20th DAY

"FLYING CLOUD"
30th DAY

"SWORDFISH"
30th DAY

SOUTH
AMERICA

"FLYING CLOUD"
40th DAY

"SWORDFISH"
40th DAY

"SWORDFISH"
60th DAY

"SWORDFISH"
BEST DAY'S RUN
325 MILES

SPECIFICATIONS		
	"FLYING CLOUD"	"SWORDFISH"
TONNAGE	1782	1036
LENGTH	229'—0"	169'—6"
WIDTH	40'—8"	36'—6"
DEPTH	21'—6"	20'—0"
CAPTAIN	JOSIAH P. CREESY	DAVID S. BABCOCK
BUILDER	DONALD McKAY EAST BOSTON, MASS.	WILLIAM H. WEBB NEW YORK, N. Y.
OWNER	GRINNEL, MINTURN & CO. NEW YORK	BARCLAY & LIVINGSTON NEW YORK

"FLYING CLOUD"
50th DAY

"SWORDFISH"
50th DAY

CAPE HORN

LATITUDE & LONGITUDE POSITIONS PLOTTED FOR EACH DAY FROM
THE ORIGINAL LOGS BY ARTHUR C. BABCOCK JANUARY 20th 1952

Cal Sacks

THE TWILIGHT OF
Sailing Ships

Robert Carse

Foreword by HOWARD I. CHAPELLE

CONSULTANTS

HOWARD I. CHAPELLE
Smithsonian Institution
U.S. National Museum

REAR ADMIRAL GORDON McLINTOCK
U.S. Merchant Service
Superintendent, U.S. Merchant Marine Academy

COMMODORE JOHN S. BAYLIS
U.S. Coast Guard, (Ret.)

GALAHAD BOOKS · NEW YORK CITY

PUBLISHED BY Galahad Books

A DIVISION OF A & W PROMOTIONAL BOOK CORPORATION

95 MADISON AVENUE, NEW YORK, N.Y. 10016

BY ARRANGEMENT WITH GROSSET & DUNLAP

LIBRARY OF CONGRESS CATALOG CARD NO.: 65-13792

ISBN: 0-88365-036-3

MANUFACTURED IN THE UNITED STATES OF AMERICA

This is for Frank O. Braynard
with gratitude
for what he has done
for all who love ships

Acknowledgments

Gʀᴀᴛɪᴛᴜᴅᴇ ᴍᴜsᴛ ʙᴇ ᴇxᴘʀᴇssᴇᴅ here for the help given me in the creation of this book. First, it goes to Commodore John S. Baylis, USCG, Ret.; to Howard I. Chapelle; and to Rear Admiral Gordon McLintock, USMS. Without their most generous assistance, the book would not have been written. Then there are:

Harold S. Sniffen, Robert H. Burgess, John L. Lochhead and the staff of the Mariners Museum, Newport News, Virginia; Charles A. Brooks, Edouard A. Stackpole and Miss Alma Eshenfelder of the Marine Historical Association, Mystic, Connecticut; C. V. Brewington and the other members of the staff of the Peabody Museum, Salem, Massachusetts; Mrs. Eleanor C. Waters, Mrs. Katherine Ketchum, Edmund F. Wagner and George D. Wintress of the Seamen's Bank for Savings, New York City; Miss Elizabeth Colman and Miss Ruth Hicklin of the Seamen's Church Institute, New York City; Miss Barbara Burrows of the United Fruit Company, Boston, Massachusetts; Frank O. Braynard and Jeff Blinn of the Moran Towing and Transportation Company, New York City; the staff of the British Information Service, New York City; the staff of the Danish Information Service, New York City; H. Ramo of the Finnish National Travel Office, New York City; the staff of the German Information Center, New York City; the staff of the Portuguese Information Office, New York City; the staff of the Spanish Chamber of Commerce, New York City; Bertram B. Lewis of the Lake Carriers Association, Cleveland, Ohio; Jon Embretsen, director of the Norwegian Information Service in New York.

And: Arthur C. Babcock, Huntington, New York; Lieutenant Commander Harry A. Hart, USMS, United States Merchant Marine Academy, Kings Point, New York; Michael Chassid, New York City; Morton B. Collins, Springfield, Massachusetts; Stephen Zoll, New York City; Robert Crandall Associates, Inc., New York City; K. V. W. Lawrence, The Compass, and Socony Mobil Oil Co., Inc.

And: Edgar Erickson, Mariehamn, Finland; F. Liewendahl, Mariehamn, Finland; Captain Eivind Ottensen, master of *Staatsrad Lehmkul;* Captain Alan Villiers, Oxford, England.

Gratitude should be expressed also for the help again given by my wife, Janet; and to Joseph Greene, my editor on this book, for his unflagging patience and energy.

R. C.

Hotel Chelsea,
New York City,
1965.

Contents

Color Plates

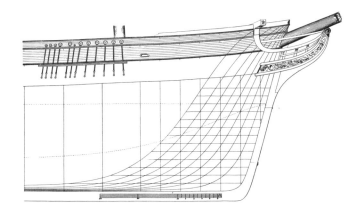

Foreword

by HOWARD I. CHAPELLE

THE LAST DAYS OF COMMERCIAL sailing vessels have rarely been discussed at length. At most, maritime historians and writers have produced short accounts of the last days of sailing packet ships or clipper ships or down-casters, confining their efforts to a single, distinguished type of sailing vessel.

Here, Robert Carse has written of the final days of many types of vessels, showing the slow decadence of the sailing freighters as a whole and their final economic death-struggles, ending with the supremacy of mechanical power at sea in case after case.

The economy of sail, in sea transportation, was a pied-piper that led many merchants to ruin. They did not realize that economy is a far ranging subject, for the costs of manpower needed only to operate a sailing freighter would eventually exceed the costs of fuel and maintenance, of interest on construction costs and of management of a mechanically propelled vessel. Even though sailing freighters might make an occasional passage in steamer time, or less, sail was outmoded. What was required was regularity of cargo delivery; a gas works needed coal every six days, on the nose, not the hit-and-miss delivery of the economical sailing collier.

There was plenty to mislead. The sailing freighters, such as the great coal schooners, were cheaper to build than steamers of the same capacity, for the whole hull of the sailing vessel could be given up to cargo with the result that a given bulk-cargo could be carried in a smaller hull than in a steamer. And the latter had to have machinery, costly stuff requiring expensive fuel. Wind cost only the sailmakers' and riggers' bills. By pinching on the size of the crew, adding deck machinery, the coal schooner and sailing bulk carrier might undercut the steam-pot all across the board.

Yes, sail looked good and many backed sail with their bankroll. But one thing alone broke the sailing freighter: irregularity of cargo delivery. What was the cause of emphasis on regularity of operation? *Inventory;* a business did not have to invest in, and assume risks for, a large inventory requiring heavy investments tied up for long periods, with loss of interest and risk of depreciation in the material stocked. With regular deliveries, inventories were brought to short term investments and the savings obtained could be invested in more productive ways.

This, then, is the back-drop of the stage on which the slow tragedy of the end of the sailing freighters, and of fishing vessels, will be played, as told in this book. Robert Carse deals with the courage, cowardice, madness and command with which the acts are played, with a touch of maritime history to tie the acts together.

Yet, when the play is done, the final end of commercial sail cannot be seen. Sailing oyster dredges exist on the Chesapeake and sailing junks are in the news from Viet Nam, the China coast and Taiwan. But the story will be the same, with the final fadeout in the creeks, bays and rivers rather than on the high seas.

———————

THE TWILIGHT OF
Sailing Ships

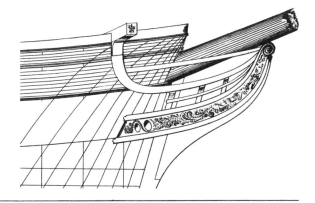

CHAPTER ONE

Clippers In Their Glory

. . . veterans now of Cape Horn, and no better sailors lived.

Twilight came very slowly, almost imperceptibly upon the sailing ships. Man had used them from before the time of recorded history. The effects of the winds, their power to move a ship over the sea, seized and held the imagination of sailors, merchants, geographers and kings for many centuries.

The very early seagoing people, the Phoenicians, had their wind gods. And the Egyptians, and the Greeks, and the Vikings. The sailors who came home from a voyage told stories which the bards picked up and made into epics.

There was the sand-harsh *simoom* that swept off the North African desert and lashed the eyes and faces of the citizens of ancient Massalia. The high-ribbed mountains behind the port gave the coast another wind, the chill, mean *mistral,* and out past the Pillars of Hercules were all the great Atlantic storms. Then, on around the globe were the Northeast trade winds, and the Southeasterlies from below the Equator; and on the Spanish Main, in among the green and steep Antilles, was the sudden, terrible cyclonic storm the Caribs called *huracano.*

When men who had sailed with Magellan came back to port, they spoke of a wind named *pampero* which blew off the Argentine plains with abrupt violence and added to the dangers of a ship headed toward the stark gray granite of Cape Horn, around the southernmost reaches of the continent. The China seas, along with the coast of what was still known as Cathay, were to be remembered for the dread *taifung.* The English translated that as typhoon, and had vivid accounts of the massive, drubbing force of the *monsoons* which the Arabs used season in, season out to sail from the Red Sea and the Arabian Gulf to Malaysia, Africa, Madagascar and back.

The beautiful medium clipper *Kirkcudbrightshire* was built in 1884 and sailed out of Glasgow, Scotland. Broken up in 1922, the ship lay as a hulk until 1927.

Men began to write books about the winds. Shipmasters compiled their own very private wind charts, plotting on them the courses their vessels should follow to make the voyage outward-bound and home as fast as possible. Knowledge of the winds and their uses attained the highest degree of concentration during the American clipper ship period of 1850-60. It was very keenly needed. Clipper ship masters reckoned the performance of their vessels in premiums that would bring thousands of dollars for each day saved on a run.

Those vessels often carried as many as thirty-three sails, which meant two acres of canvas spread aloft. Aboard the most extreme of their class, the mainmast truck stood 200 feet above the deck. Men have not built or sailed such ships since; they are forever gone. But for many years after their economic purpose was proven to be past, the challenge of their beauty, grace and speed persisted.

The departure of a clipper like *Lightning, Flying Cloud,* or *Rainbow* from her East River pier in the Port of New York in the 1850's was an unforgettable sight. The usual custom was to bring the ship down from her loading berth and anchor her off Castle Garden, at the foot of Manhattan. The owners boarded there for a glass of sherry and a final word with the captain. Then they went ashore, and the anchor catted, a tall-stacked tug on the tow-line, the ship took the ebb tide and started for the Lower Bay, Sandy Hook and the open sea.

Most of the captains made an inflexible habit of wearing their shore-going clothing, stove pipe hats and all, until the vessels were well away from the land. The mates handled the work down on deck, and the sailors, those of them who were sober enough to understand orders, climbed aloft to the yards and unbent canvas.

16

A wet day aboard the Norwegian *Sorlandet* as the modern training ship bucks hard to choppy seas in the North Atlantic. Below, a cadet holds her carefully on course.

"A Yankee clipper with a Yankee skipper" was a common sight in Caribbean ports. In the foreground, the bumboat folks get ready to row alongside the clipper to sell fresh fruit, rum and other goods to the crew.

The great, lean ship spread her sails one after the other, and the helmsman, with the sharp gaze of the master upon him, put her squarely on course. The topsails were set first, and the jibs, then the topgallantsails. The big courses came last, and if the weather held fair, the royals and studdingsails were added to her driving force.

Wind drummed upon the white, fine American duck that curved taut beneath the yards and from the stays. The braces, the tacks and sheets hummed with the strain. The shrouds talked, too, and the masts. The waves lifted, dipped, struck the ship, rushed on aft along her runs with an ardent splatter of foam.

The captain left the poop after a while and turned over the ship to the first mate. He went below to his cabin and took off the shore-going finery, dressed in a woolen jersey and bell-bottomed trousers, China-side straw slippers. Then, in the case beside the chart table in the saloon, he stowed his chronometers and his sextant. He made the first entries of the voyage in his logbook, giving the time of departure and the distance and bearing from the land when it was taken. He unfurled his Atlantic chart and laid off the rhumb line course that would best serve the ship on her voyage to Cape Horn at the Southernmost tip of South America. It was a long haul ahead, and he did not welcome it. The ship would reach the Cape Horn region during the Antarctic winter, make her westing among icebergs and against furious gales. The captain grunted in anticipation of the inevitable Cape Horn misery, put the chart away and went to bed.

The clipper ran smartly South, cleared the Horse Latitudes—the belt of calms

"Across the Atlantic..."   *Great Western* of the Black Ball Line   Painting by Antonio Jacobsen

"Near twilight..."   East River, 1894   Painting by Charles Robert Patterson

With Alcatraz Island rising in the background, the extreme clipper *Senator* unloads her cargo at the Chestnut Street wharf in San Francisco. This remarkable photograph was taken in 1866.

bordering the Equator—caught the Southeast trades, hauled her braces sharp up and kept heading for the Cape. Her daily runs averaged around three hundred miles. She was a well-found ship. The watches even sang a chanty as they yanked at the pump handles in the morning before they turned to with holy-stones, deck swabs and the salt water hose. The captain paced the poop alone, proud, remote, a figure the sailors had come to respect, and, in a sense, fear.

It was the captain who would make the fateful decisions off Cape Horn. He owned the absolute authority to send all hands aloft in the middle of a black and screaming night. If he so wished, he could keep upper canvas spread until topmasts snapped, spars and sails thrashed beyond control, and men were killed or drowned.

The young sailors tightened their belts as they listened to the old-timers' stories. They wiped the sweat from the palms of their hands on their dungarees. Then, once more, they looked high aloft where the royal yards swung in erratic arcs across the sky. There were no more chanties in the morning when the ship reached 50 degrees South latitude and squared away for the westward traverse into the Pacific. Men talked about very little except ship's work. This before them was the supreme test for any sailor.

Aboard a clipper ship bound for California in the days of the Gold Rush of 1849. Fair weather brought the passengers out on deck for some fresh air and sunshine.

When it was achieved, when the ship had beaten through into the Pacific, the young, green hands in the crew felt a new confidence in themselves. They were veterans now of Cape Horn, and no better sailors lived. It gave them great pride in spite of the torture of frostbite, sea boils, weeks of cold food, wet clothes and sodden bunks.

The clipper ship crews realized that competition was extremely sharp, that their jobs might not last, and could soon be taken from them by more prosaic vessels. Sturdy, broad-beamed packet ships, big cargo carriers, dominated a lot of the trans-atlantic trade and kept regular schedules with European ports and Boston, New York and Baltimore. The packets were also active in the passenger business, moving European emigrants westward by the thousands. Sailing vessels of all sorts, among them the powerful square-riggers designed on less extreme lines than the clipper, and the schooners, and the increasingly popular steamers were another menace. But as long as a clipper could run her 300 miles and better a day, she was still queen of the seas, the finest vessel afloat.

The lure of gold proved too strong for the men aboard ships coming into San Francisco. This early daguerrotype shows the harbor crowded with ships abandoned by their crews.

Carrying both her topsails and all her other canvas, an unidentified American schooner enters Havana harbor. Morro Castle is on her port bow. This stereotype dates back to 1860.

Clipper ship *Gamecock* leaving the harbor at Whampoa, China, with a cargo of tea.

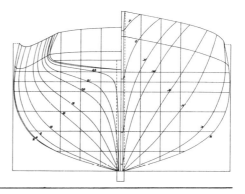

CHAPTER TWO

The Captains' Wives

. . . I grew very fond of this sea life.

For centuries, the mothers of New England seagoing families had known of the death toll to be taken. Where two strong boys sat at breakfast in their Cape Cod kitchen, a mother could tell herself with absolute, chill certainty that one of the pair would not survive. He would be placed on the list of missing from a deepwater ship, or a schooner, or lose his life while hauling lobster pots in the tide rips of the bay.

The pain of such knowledge, and of the years of separation from their husbands, was too much for a number of the women to accept. Whenever they could, those lucky enough to be captains' wives went to sea with their men. Mrs. Charlotte Babcock, wife of Captain David S. Babcock, master of the famous extreme clipper *Swordfish,* was among the first, in 1851. The custom persisted through the Down Easter period and the days of the big schooners. Mrs. Babcock was a young woman when she joined her husband aboard *Swordfish,* and she brought with her their nine months old daughter, Nellie, and Nellie's nurse.

Captain Babcock, a Stonington man and a crack sailor, was determined to beat the record established a few months before by *Flying Cloud.* But his vessel was considerably smaller than the other. William H. Webb had designed *Swordfish,* and her specifications of 1,036 tons, an over all length of 169.5 feet and a 36.5 foot beam meant she carried much less sail. It was almost universal opinion along New York's South Street that Babcock did not have a chance.

PAINTING BY GORDON GRANT

Flying Cloud, the greatest clipper of them all, performing in the kind of weather she liked. Her best day's run was 374 sea miles.

A model of *Flying Cloud* shows her graceful lines.

He had in his possession, though, a copy of the *Flying Cloud* log made on her record-breaking voyage. He spent long hours in discussion with Lieutenant Matthew F. Maury, USN, before he took *Swordfish* to sea. The lieutenant was an international authority on winds and currents, and had compiled from thousands of deepwater ships' log books his "Sailing Directions" and "Wind and Current Charts." When Captain Babcock cleared for San Francisco on November 11, 1851, he held invaluable information.

Mrs. Babcock, her daughter Nellie given over to the care of the nurse most of the time, was able to keep her own private record of the voyage. Her husband was delighted that she, the nurse and the child all proved themselves reasonably free from seasickness after the first few days out. Mrs. Babcock found her quarters comfortable and well-appointed. She wrote:

"We had a splendid run off the coast, with a strong fair wind, and although I was seasick at first, I was not very much so and on the third day was able to go on deck a while but was very glad to go below again. I shall never forget the wonderful sight, nothing but the sky above and the water beneath, as far as the eye could see, and the immense waves following each other in unbroken succession, which as they came toward us, it seemed impossible for us to escape being overwhelmed by them and it was all so new and strange to me, but as the Captain explained, and I soon saw, the ship rose to the occasion and went over easily and gracefully, showing herself thus early a fine sailer, and, as she afterward proved, a very fast one, for we made the voyage around Cape Horn in ninety days 18 hours and it had never been done before

A studdingsail serves to advertise the next voyage of the *Flying Cloud*. As much as $60 a ton was charged for premium cargo, but the hold space was small due to her concave hull construction.

in that time except by one ship. Capt. Cressy of ship *Flying Cloud* made it in ninety days.

"It seemed so wonderful to go on deck day after day and see nothing but this vast expanse of water and sky, and ourselves apparently the only living things in the world, for we rarely saw a vessel of any kind, but I soon became accustomed to it and the motion of the ship, and as the weather grew warmer enjoyed sitting on deck watching the sailors at their work, but it was a long time before I could bear to see them go aloft to furl a sail or do other necessary work, and it has always been a wonder to me that so few comparatively meet with serious accidents. In all of the seven years that I was at sea, I only remember one, a sailor who fell from aloft one dark night and was never seen afterwards although a long search was made."

Swordfish, besides her high-premium cargo, was carrying passengers to San Francisco. There were six staterooms for passenger accomodation in the after part of the vessel, and they were all occupied. But Mrs. Babcock had little to do with them, and wrote in her journal:

"As it was in the early days of the discovery of gold in California, we had several passengers bound for that El Dorado to seek their fortunes, but as none of them was especially interesting, in fact the reverse, I shall not describe them, and after leaving San Francisco never heard of them again."

Mrs. Babcock, as was her privilege as wife of the master of the vessel, remained aloof. She was entering a new world, and wanted nothing to disturb it:

"I grew very fond of this sea life (after conquering my fear of the waves) and

The sort of home a clipper captain's wife left when she sailed with her husband. This eighteenth century house and adjoining chapel face the water at The Seaport, Mystic, Connecticut.

my chief delight was to sit on deck with my husband on pleasant evenings watching the waves and the ever changing sky and talking of home and friends and singing old familiar songs, and my days were always occupied with my baby, my sewing or a book so that the time never seemed tedious or monotonous to me, being always happy and contented.

"We had pleasant weather on that first voyage, and the Captain was in high spirits over the sailing of the ship. He had good officers and crew, and as I developed such good sailing qualities, and the nurse and baby also, he felt a great satisfaction in having taken us with him, as at first it seemed a great responsibility, and it was under all the circumstances, so we had many happy hours together and the time passed swiftly by.

"The forty-seventh day out from New York, the glad cry of "Land Ho" was heard from the mast-head and all rushed on deck to see it.

"It proved to be the long, low desolate looking coast of Tierra del Fuego, not far from Cape Horn, and though destitute of any signs of vegetation or habitation, still it was land, and therefore an object of interest. As we sailed nearer, it looked still more desolate and dreary, with only a few seagulls flying about and the waves dashing on the rocky shore. The weather was clear and very mild, it being the last of December, consequently the summer season there and having a fair wind we passed the extreme point of Cape Horn, with all sails set and studding sails also, a most remarkable experience as anyone familiar with that latitude can testify. I sat on deck and made sketches of the different points.

"After passing the Cape and getting into the Pacific Ocean, we rang the changes on the weather, having the usual variety, head winds and fair, rain and fog, and occasionally a calm, much to the disgust of the Captain, who could bear with equa-

The dining room of the same house, with pewter ware in the corner cabinet.

A prosperous sea captain could decorate his living room with such splendid wall paper, usually brought over from England.

nimity anything but that, as he was very anxious to beat the record of the *Flying Cloud* mentioned before and up to the 85th day we were several days ahead of the time (we had an abstract of her log and so could follow her course exactly) when, alas, the wind came out dead ahead and not much of it, and therefore we had to beat the rest of the way and our passage was 21 hours longer than hers."

With this simple language, Mrs. Babcock described what must have been a deeply agonizing experience for her husband. The master of *Swordfish,* in his tremendous desire to defeat *Flying Cloud,* brought his vessel closer to land than Lieutenant Maury had recommended for the last day's run. He met fitful head winds that set him badly back. Captain Cressy had taken *Flying Cloud* past the San Francisco headlands on a brisk Southeast breeze.

But, despite the poor sailing at the end of the passage, Captain Babcock established a remarkable record. It was registered as the fourth fastest passage ever made, and the best performance by any ship built in New York. The ship rid of San Francisco cargo and passengers, Captain Babcock, his wife, Nellie, and the nurse, kept on to China to load tea for home. Mrs. Babcock was to have many more strange sights, scenes and events to enter in her journal, and to relate afterwards to her neighbors in Stonington.

Mrs. Cressy, the wife of the master of *Flying Cloud,* was at sea the same time as Mrs. Babcock, but in a much different capacity. Captain Cressy had taught her early in their marriage how to navigate, and she left their home in Marblehead and joined him. She sailed with him continuously and relieved him and the mate of the difficult navigational duties, allowing them more time on deck for ship handling. She used a big English sextant made by Dent, the Bowditch five-place logarithm tables, several chronometers, and a complicated method of finding position that occupied a full foolscap page with figures. Her work was highly satisfactory, and Captain Cressy who checked it regularly to establish his day's run, seldom found corrections necessary.

During a voyage that followed the 1851 record-breaking New York-San Francisco run, *Flying Cloud* was bound for Madagascar in heavy weather. Mrs. Cressy was alone in the main cabin where she worked at the chart table to plot the ship's line of position. When she looked up to rest her eyes and stared out of the sunlit port-hole above her, she saw in the foam of a wave crest the flash of a sailor's bare feet as he tumbled aft, hopelessly submerged. He had fallen from aloft while at some job in the rigging, Mrs. Cressy knew, and must be already half-conscious from shock.

She went fast up the companionway ladder onto the poop, gave at once the cry, "Man overboard!"

A life-ring was tossed, and Captain Cressy took the ship immediately off the wind, sending a boat away with the mate in charge. The boat came back about an hour before dusk. The mate reported bad luck: no sign of the man at all. Mrs. Cressy talked with her husband. She indicated the wind drift, and the direction in which the man had probably floated. She knew that after darkness the boat crew would also be

A ship's galley where the cook sweated out his chores in fair weather or foul.

The officers' saloon where the captain and his mates took their meals.

in great danger and might not be able to regain the ship. Captain Cressy agreed, then ordered another boat put in the water and manned under command of the second mate. He wanted both boats, he said, to keep searching until the last possible moment of daylight.

The man was found in the dusk by one of the boats, so weak he could not yell any more, or kick up a wake against the sharks that had begun to surround him. He was hauled aboard, covered in a blanket, and taken to *Flying Cloud,* where he became Mrs. Cressy's patient. Captain Cressy worked at the navigation for the next few days, and after *Flying Cloud* reached port and the story was told, Mrs. Cressy became famous in sailor bars and boarding-houses all around the world.

There were other captains' wives, though, who distinguished themselves a great deal more than Mrs. Cressy. Records of what they did are only partial, have been lost in the intervening years, or at best were no more than a series of log book entries, a short article on the maritime page of a newspaper after the safe arrival of the vessel in port.

The history of the American extreme clipper *Neptune's Car* and the achievement of Mrs. Patten, the wife of the master, is sorely incomplete. Still, it is known that in the 1850 period of hard-driving passages for California, the ship was bound around Cape Horn when the mate proved insubordinate. Captain Patten was forced to confine the mate to his room, and take over the officer's duties. The consequent strain was too much. Captain Patten developed brain fever; he lay unconscious, gravely ill.

The second mate lacked any knowledge of navigation. If *Neptune's Car* was to make her Cape Horn westing, Mrs. Patten must handle the work unaided. She was

31

nineteen years old at the time, had been married when she was sixteen, and had been sea-going with her husband ever since. She checked her husband's work book for the last celestial sights he had taken, went up on deck with his sextant, plotted her sights, established the new position of the ship, told the second mate what course to steer, and what sails should be kept aloft. *Neptune's Car* came into San Francisco like that, with a much better than average run.

The tradition lasted. When the American clipper *Frank N. Thayer* was homeward-bound with a cargo of jute from Manila to New York in January, 1886 there was sudden, savage mutiny. Two Filipino sailors who had been shipped in Manila went berserk in the middle of the night. With their sharp-bladed *bolos,* they killed in rapid succession the wheelsman and both mates, and then seriously wounded Captain Clark, the master, and four sailors.

Mrs. Clark was aboard with her small child. She realized at once the gravity of what had happened. The ship lay aback to her canvas, helmless, 700 miles from St. Helena in the South Atlantic. Mrs. Clark secured her child in the captain's cabin, then managed to reach her husband, bring him his revolver, and bind up his wounds.

Captain Clark, revolver in one hand, bull's-eye lantern in the other, mustered the survivors of the crew. He shot and wounded one of the Filipinos when the man refused orders. But the other crazed sailor ducked away in the darkness, pried open a corner of the fore hatch, went below into the hold and set the tinder-dry jute cargo afire.

The fire spread so fast that Captain Clark, with the few men left to him, could do nothing but abandon ship. Mrs. Clark put her baby in the lifeboat that was to be used, risked her life again to return to the main cabin for her husband's sextant, a chart, a chronometer and a set of navigation tables. There would be weeks of sailing in the open boat to get to St. Helena, the only possible landfall.

Fire was in the rigging and the sails when Mrs. Clark came on deck and took her place in the boat beside her child and her husband. Topmasts were about to topple out of the ship, and she blazed in all her length. But the pair of Filipinos had slipped a small spar over the side, clung to it as the lifeboat was lowered and paddled past them.

Captain Clark was supported on the boat's stern thwart by his wife. He took careful aim and killed both men. There was no time left for mercy. The boat lacked a sail, and she was encumbered by the wounded, and the child. Those who were able to move paddled her beyond the blazing wreckage of the ship. Mrs. Clark was grateful for the light it gave; she stitched up blankets into a sail. Then the sail was hoisted, and the voyage begun for St. Helena on a course laid off by Captain Clark.

The boat with all hands safe aboard entered Jamestown harbor in St. Helena at midnight, January 10, 1886. Port authorities notified J. A. McKnight, the American consul, and he came out to meet the boat's people along with a doctor. He offered his home to Captain and Mrs. Clark and their baby, then congratulated the parents upon their great good luck, their seamanship and courage.

The full-rigged British ship *Mount Stewart* was home for Mrs. M.C. McColm, the master's wife, for thirteen years. Her two sons were born on board the ship.

The masters of British medium clippers also took their wives to sea with them as often as possible, and in the last period of service for the ships, after 1900, several women shared the long, slow voyages. The ships were in ballast a lot of the time, and shuttled back and forth around the world after cargo. But the half dozen or so that remained under the British flag had become a sailor's dream, "a home away from home," and most of the crews knew no other life except under sail.

This was particularly true of the 1,903 ton steel-hulled *Mount Stewart,* built in 1891 as a full-rigged ship for the Australian wool trade. When she was finally sold to the ship-breakers in 1925, her master, M. C. McColm, had been in command for seventeen years, and he had never worked aboard a steamer. The sail-maker had been in the ship for sixteen years, the cook for eleven, and some of the able-bodied sailors nearly as long. Captain McColm's wife, an Australian, had sailed steadily with him for a little over thirteen years, and in that time had given birth to two sons.

Captain McColm went to live in New South Wales, Australia, when he took down his flag from *Mount Stewart.* He bought a dairy farm at his wife's urging. Their sons found the life quite interesting, because they had never lived in a house, and had seen cows in pasture only at a distance.

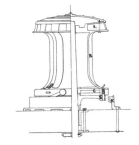

CHAPTER THREE

Decline of the Clippers

. . . in the midst of festivities, the proof of doom.

THE COURAGE AND SKILL of the men who sailed the swift, graceful clippers were not enough to stave off the inevitable. Three signs clearly indicated the future, and warned that wind-driven ships could not continue to dominate the sea trade. The first was the successful run, in 1809, of the steamer *Phenix* from Hoboken to Philadelphia, down the Atlantic coast. The second was the establishment by Samuel Cunard of a regular steamer service from Halifax to Boston, then across the Atlantic to Liverpool, England. This Cunard achieved by 1840, after improvement of the machinery used aboard the *Phenix* and on British-flag steamers maintained in the Irish Sea traffic.

Boston merchants, delighted with the profits that steam might bring them, made Cunard guest of honor at several champagne banquets, and even paid for a tug to break a channel through the ice for one of his steamers when Massachusetts Bay froze over. The same group of merchants, though, kept investing in, or buying, extreme clippers of the kind built by Donald McKay in his East Boston yard. Steamers, they said, were really "stink pots," and were infested with riffraff Liverpool Irish firemen, and a great part of the potential cargo space was taken up by coal bunkers. And why buy coal when all the winds of the world were there to move a ship? Besides, tea carried in steamers had a coal smoke flavor when the cargoes arrived from the Orient. Only in sailing vessels was the flavor fully retained, unblemished. Then the dubious, those who thought steamers might win out somehow, were told to recall the history of *Savannah*. When she was built in 1819, she was supposed to be a definite threat to sailing ships. But the steamer on her maiden voyage to the United Kingdom used her sails a great deal more than her paddle wheels.

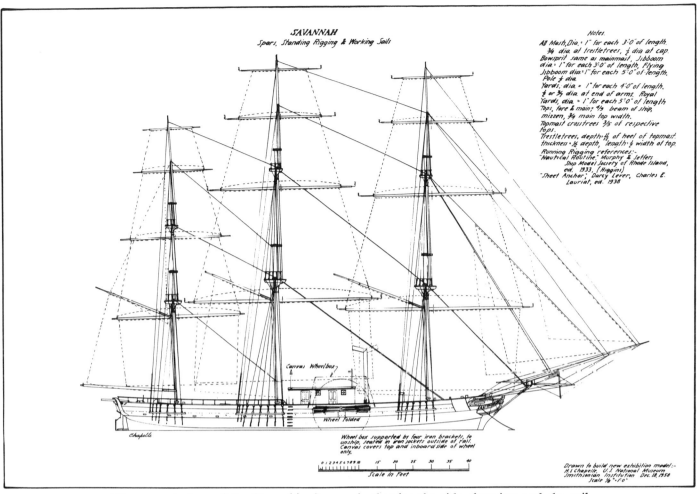

SAVANNAH
Spars, Standing Rigging & Working Sails

Canvas Wheelbox

Wheel Folded

Wheel box supported by four iron brackets, to
unship, seated in iron sockets outside of rail.
Canvas covers top and inboard side of wheel
only.

Chapelle

0 1 2 3 4 5 6 7 8 9 10   15   20   25   30   35   40
Scale in Feet

Notes.
All Mast, Dia. = 1" for each 3'0" of length.
¾ dia. at trestletrees, ½ dia at cap.
Bowsprit same as mainmast, Jibboom
dia. = 1" for each 3'0" of length, Flying
Jibboom dia = 1" for each 5'0" of length.
Pole ½ dia.
Yards, dia. = 1" for each 4'0" of length.
¼ or ¾ dia. at end of arms, Royal
Yards, dia = 1" for each 5'0" of length
Tops, fore & main = ⅓ beam of ship,
mizzen, ¾ main top width.
Topmast crosstrees ⅔ of respective
tops.
Trestletrees, depth = ½ of heel of topmast,
thickness = ⅛ depth, length = ⅞ width of top.
Running Rigging references:-
"Nautical Routine", Murphy & Jeffers
Ship Model Society of Rhode Island,
ed. 1933, (Higgins)
"Sheet Anchor", Darcy Lever, Charles E.
Lauriat, ed. 1938

Drawn to build new exhibition model:-
H.I. Chapelle, U.S. National Museum
Smithsonian Institution Dec. 18, 1958
Scale ¾" = 1'0"

The correct plans of the Steamship *Savannah*, showing the side elevation and the sail plan, found after many years of careful research. These plans were drawn to architectural scale by Howard I. Chapelle.

This model, built from unverified information, was used for many years in textbooks and various exhibits.

The true model of the *Savannah*, showing the different smokestack and paddle-wheels that could be folded back when not in use.

PAINTING BY J. LYNN, 1826

The paddle steamer *Shannon* using both sails and steam to make her way to a port through heavy weather. The smoke and steam from the valve on the smokestack show that the stokers are keeping up the pressure.

The third sign that doomed sail, regardless of the continued and quite fanatical enthusiasm for it, was very evident when the superb clipper *Flying Cloud* came into New York in April, 1852, having made good the unparalleled record of 374 nautical miles sailed in a day. Her owners were the famous shipping firm, Grinnell, Minturn & Co. They were extremely proud of the ship's achievement. Her log was printed in gold on white silk for distribution to their friends at a gala reception at the Astor House. They also exhibited at the reception the topmast fids—solid pieces of oak wedged in to hold the mast firm—taken from *Flying Cloud* after she reached port.

These closely fitted pieces of oak had been macerated nearly into pulp by the action of the vessel while under a press of canvas at sea. It was not difficult for anybody who knew the rudiments of ship construction to realize that, if the topmast fids were chewed apart, there must have been equally severe and excessive strain on all parts of the vessel. The clippers were of wood construction. They could not possibly hold up as seaworthy with the stresses of the Cape Horn gales, the weeks of beating against the China Sea monsoons, the long, bitter Pacific battering. Right here in the Astor House, in the midst of the festivities, the owners of *Flying Cloud* had shown how short-lived the vessels of her kind would be, if driven at a speed to bring home profitable cargoes.

The dubious, when they spoke of this, were quickly answered. It was pointed out to them that Donald McKay took only 60 days to build the extreme clipper *Stag Hound*. She made on her first voyage to California and China in 1851 enough to pay for herself, and a profit of $80,000 for her owners, Sampson and Tappan.

But William H. Webb, the astute New York shipbuilder, in the peak year of 1853 when more than fifty clippers were launched, decided that he would stop construction of the type. He gave over the work in his East River yard to the building of steamships, vessels of war, and some packets of conventional, "old-fashioned" sailing ship design. Medium clippers were built after 1853; and no extreme clippers at all after 1855.

Webb was completely right in his estimate of the need for change. By the end of 1853, it was obvious that there were not sufficient cargoes for all the fine new, heavily rigged clippers. Cargo rates had been as high as $60 a ton at the peak of the California 1849-50 boom. Now they were much lower, and just about what an owner would accept to keep his vessel active. McKay's winner, *Flying Cloud,* was idle for two and a half years as her agents hunted ladings for her, and they were finally glad to take $10 a ton for San Francisco freight.

The final blow was dealt the clippers in 1854-5 when the Panama Railroad across the Isthmus was finished and opened. There was no more Cape Horn thrash for the skysail-yarders, for the men who built the railroad put into operation a fleet of steamers that operated from Panama northward to San Francisco, and at premium passenger and cargo rates.

McKay, a stubborn Scot with dreams he refused to relinquish, kept on building clippers. He was determined, in spite of the advice of his friends, to build the biggest of them all. Her name was *Great Republic,* her length 335 feet, her tonnage 4,555. The

Using steam power to aid her sails, the Confederate raider *Alabama* strains to elude United States Navy frigates.

An early photograph shows one of the attempts to compromise between steam power and sail. The *Kite* is wooden-hulled and square-rigged with a tremendous bowsprit and jibboom that gives her almost clipper proportions.

bankers and the merchants were skeptical of her and refused to invest. McKay built her with his own money, and lost when she was swept by fire as she lay at a New York yard waiting for the final rigging work.

There were other ships for McKay to build. He went on to construct for James Baines, the Scottish shipowner, some of his most lovely sharp-lined clippers. He experimented also with iron hulls, and iron frames that took wooden planking. Then, in desperation, and almost financially ruined, he built several steamers. It was the end for him. He retired to a Massachusetts farm, inland from the sea.

Twilight had obscured the dreams that had been with him since boyhood. He was not bitter as he recognized that the ships which he had designed and whose beauty was unmatched were, after a span of ten years, no longer wanted in international trade. But he felt rejected, thrust aside, and made to seem almost ridiculous.

Donald McKay died in the midst of his family, respected and deeply loved by them and hundreds of friends. But he could not have had much reluctance about meeting death. His life had really finished back on that wind-filled, brilliant day when *Flying Cloud* logged 374 sea miles.

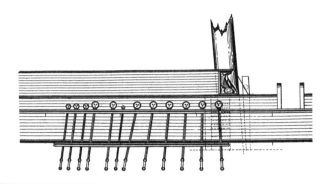

CHAPTER FOUR

The Cape Horn Gamble

. . . lost main topsail yard, and main and mizzen topgallant masts.

THE SEVERE FINANCIAL DEPRESSION in the United States during 1856-7 collapsed the last, lingering dreams of the clipper ship owners. They could no longer afford the Cape Horn gamble. Steamers carried the California cargoes, for what they were worth, and at much lower insurance rates for the shipper. Chinese tea was still being drunk in large quantities, but the public refused to quibble about "smoke taint" or "mildew" because of the iron hulls. At the Portuguese colony of Macao, and at Whampoa in the Pearl River below Canton, China, the steamers got the pick of the new crop for European, British and American consumption.

The partners in Grinnell, Minturn & Co., pinched by the depression, got out the first voyage log book for *Flying Cloud* and studied it with extreme care. Captain Joseph Perkins Cressy, the master of the vessel, had made his entries in a fine and flowing hand that was easily read. The log revealed at once the almost unbelievable damage *Flying Cloud* had suffered as Cressy forced her along the New York-San Francisco road around Cape Horn.

The entry for June 6, 1851 stated: "Lost main topsail yard, and main and mizen topgallant masts."

This was only three days after leaving New York, and Cressy kept right on, desperately forcing her. He wrote on June 11: "Very severe thunder and lightning. Double-reefed topsails. Latter part, blowing a hard gale, close-reefed topsails, split fore and main-topmast staysails.

"At 1 p.m. discovered mainmast had sprung. Sent down royal and topgallant yards and studding sail booms off lower and topsail yards to relieve the mast.

"Heavy sea running and shipping large quantities of water over lee rail."

Then, on June 14: "Discovered mainmast badly sprung about a foot from the hounds (the supports for the topmast) and fished it."

The launching of the splendid six-masted schooner *Edward B. Winslow* at Bath, Maine, in 1908. Built for hard use and great cargo capacity, she sailed the Atlantic Coast route for many years, hauling all sorts of bulk cargo, including timber, coal, granite and cement, often dangerously overloaded.

Cressy never stopped crowding her. He sent her smashing into thirty-and-forty foot seas that combed her from the cutwater piece on aft to the break of the poop and left the main deck a white, life-snatching welter. He made a log entry on July 13:— "At 6 p.m. carried away main-topsail tye and truss band around mainmast. Single-reefed topsails."

It meant that the ship could not use her main topsail, a very important sail, and that at any instant the topsail yard and the gear, weighing tons, might fall on deck. That would crush to death anybody beneath, and in all likelihood bring total disaster to the vessel by penetrating her hull or dismasting her.

Cressy was a superlative seaman, without doubt one of the finest clipper ship masters. He brought *Flying Cloud* through the gale, renewed all damage, and broke the speed record. But it was certainly not the cheapest way to handle a commercial cargo ship. The Grinnell, Minturn partners, looking over the neat log book pages, realized that, and before the depression was finished, sold *Flying Cloud*. They wanted under their house flag ships that made money.

Her new owners sent her to London in December, 1859 to pick up cargo. Captain Winsor, her master, was also a real sail-crowder, and he took advantage of the boisterous westerly gales. His time from Sandy Hook to Deal was seventeen days, an amazing record for any sailing ship.

Then *Flying Cloud* went in the keenly competitive trade to the Orient, and while she made some quick runs for her owners, she was again proven to be an unsatisfactory cargo-carrier. She leaked from the repeated beatings she had received; her heavy gear and immense spread of canvas were expensive to renew, and like all McKay ships, she was only fast in almost gale force winds. She was put upon the sales list in Hong Kong, and finally taken off it under charter to the British government to serve as transport and bring troops home.

She was offered for sale again on April 20, 1862 when she arrived in the Thames. This time she went to James Baines, the canny Liverpool shipowner, who had a fancy for McKay's designs. He put her in the Australian emigrant trade and left her there until the early 1870's, when she was once more sold. She was weary, sodden, and sorely sprung. Her fate was to carry timber in the North Atlantic trade, where she joined a great number of once famous wooden-hulled sailing vessels.

Flying Cloud piled up on the rocky New Brunswick coast in 1874, was not hauled off for some time and only after she had struck so hard that she took water in her holds and partially submerged. She was pumped out, refloated, and towed to St. John for repairs. But while in the shipyard there fire broke out aboard her. It was the end for her; the ship was not worth the repair bill. She was broken up for the copper sheathing and the other metal in her, and that was sold for junk.

Most of the public, the four terrible years of the Civil War between them and the great era of the clipper ships, had already forgotten *Flying Cloud*. But the ship-builders in Maine, in Newburyport, Massachusetts, and in Mystic, along the narrow

The 4-masted *Roanoke* being launched at the A. Sewall and Company yard, Bath, Maine, in 1892. Ships built in Maine practically dominated the coastal trade.

Mystic River in Connecticut, remembered her very well, and gained a lesson from the extremity of her design. It had been the proud boast of the Grinnell, Minturn people at the outset of *Flying Cloud's* service that, "What she can't carry, she must drag."

The post-war American square-rigger designers saw nothing but empty boasting in that statement, and went ahead to build medium clippers. The British were also building similar vessels, although they had put down several extreme clippers such as the famous, beautiful and fast *Cutty Sark* and *Thermopylae*. These were constructed for the China tea trade, and for the long hauls out and back to Australia. British clipper ship business had been stimulated by the Australian gold rush of 1857, and maintained by carrying emigrants outward-bound to New Zealand and wool cargoes on the homeward run.

The American shipbuilders had to meet great competition in the international market, but they refused to put down any vessels that resembled the early clippers. They designed instead a class that came to be known as "Down Easters," and proved to be seaworthy, fast enough, and, above all, profitable when operated against the steadily growing steamer fleets. Their main purpose was to haul California grain around Cape Horn to the East Coast, and their real designation was that of medium clippers.

They got their name from the fact that nearly all of them were built in Bath and Searsport and Rockport, Maine, and in East Boston and Newburyport, in Massachusetts, and in Mystic and Stonington, in Connecticut. Then other Maine seaport towns, Damariscotta, Thomaston, Yarmouth, Frankfort, Richmond, Phippsburg, Camden, New Castle, Waldoboro, Kennebunk and Kennebunkport, expanded their shipyards and began construction of the Down Easter type.

It was strict tradition that every Boston ship be nicely finished, with a handsome and carefully carved figure-head and trail boards, and semi-elliptical stern. But the Down Easters were designed as bulk carriers. They were given square sterns, and many of them were box-sided, and there was little done about ornamentation. The owners wanted one thing: dry and safely carried cargo, with enough shifting boards and substantially built ceilings in the holds to withstand the effects of the Cape Horn gales.

During the boom period of the California gold rush, many Maine farmers had become shipwrights almost overnight. Their lack of skill was shown in the ships left to rot on the San Francisco mud flats. They went back to the farms, though, and the men who stayed on and built the Down Easters for twenty-five years after the Civil War were highly skilled, keenly aware of the standards that had been set long ago in local yards, and which they were proud to accept as a challenge to their own, personal ability.

History stretched back vividly and unbrokenly in the Maine seaport villages,

Beached broadside by storm, the full-rigged ship *Peter Rickmers* lies almost a total wreck at Fire Island, New York. Built in 1889 at Port Glasgow by Russell & Co., the ship was German owned when she went aground, May 1, 1908. She had just left New York with a cargo of case oil for Rangoon.

43

The six-masted schooner *Wyoming* coming off the ways in 1909, her decks crowded with guests. Though it was obvious that there was little future value for these ships, shipyards in Maine continued to build them. The *Wyoming* joined the rest of the Atlantic coastwise fleet carrying bulk cargo at cheap rates.

into the earliest of colonial times in the seventeenth century, the French and Indian wars, and the Revolution. The villages were very much the same as when they had been rebuilt after the last Indian or British burning: the hip-roofed white houses bright in neat, tight rows against the somber immensity of the forest, the fast-running river, the bay below the wharves, the fish sheds, and the shipyards.

Tawny yellow Tibetan rugs were on the living room floors in some of the houses. Clipper ship masters had brought them home, and chests made of camphorwood, or mango, with broad brass hasps and locks. There were ormulu clocks, and embroidered fire screens, and chandeliers that caught the afternoon sunlight and cast reflections upon the panelled walls. Right into the 1870's and '80's, mothers told their daughters how, when they were small, they had stood upon the widows' walks of these houses and watched the clippers come in from the sea. The royals were hauled up first as the captains manouvered to anchor, and then the lower topgallants were taken in, and the courses were clewed, and hoisted in the buntlines.

The men who built the Down Easters remembered these and other stories that strongly connected them to the past. They could name off the famous deepwater masters whom the little town of Searsport had supplied in the 1870's. The town had sent 70 percent of all masters into American merchant marine ships during that period. The best known among the captains were William Parse, Ned Myers, Amos Nichols, William Goodell, Benjamin F. Colcord, William R. Gilkey, and Nathan Gilkey, and several more of the Nichols family, and Henry Curtis, Joseph Sweetser, and Andrew Ross.

Searsport had twelve shipyards along six miles of waterfront. The ships she built were comparatively small, though, around 1,500 tons. The town was noted more for the men she sent to sea as mates and masters. The Down Easter shipbuilders who were prominent in the trade were Arthur Sewall, and Flint, and Chapman, Goss, Sawyer, and Packard at Bath; Samuel Walters and Edward O'Brien at Thomaston; Thompson at Kennebunk; Pascal at Camden; the Blanchard brothers at Yarmouth; Minott at Phippsburg; Reed at Waldoboro; Soule at Freeport; and there were others, all down the Maine coast, and into Massachusetts and Connecticut.

Shares in the vessels were owned in the classical way, by "locals," people in the towns where the ship was built. But the vessels were handled by New York or Boston brokers who secured the cargo charters. Cape Horn voyages cost a lot; to renew wear and tear upon hulls, rigging, gear and sails averaged $25,000 a year for a 2,000 ton vessel. This meant that she was very well kept, and that her crew were happy in her.

The men who served in the crews were usually of local stock, and connected one way or another by marriage with the mates and the master. They worked hard, ate sea biscuit that they called "bread" and which was made of California flour. Instead of the customary "salt horse" beef given in other American-flag ships and foreign vessels, they had preserved meats contained in cans called "airtights." The owners were perfectly willing to put decent stores aboard, and pay the crews well in comparison with

Typical of the times, the schooner *Lucy Evelyn* uses all available space for carrying money-earning cargo. Often the helmsman could barely see over the deck cargo.

steamer wages of about thirty dollars a month for able-bodied sailors. The owners made on their investment in a Down Easter an average of 15-20 percent.

Construction of the vessels was almost completely of native woods. The frame of a ship, her stem and stern post, breast-hooks and carlines were of white oak. The outside planking and the inside were of pitch pine, and this was also used in the deck beams, the keelson and the keel. Both keelson and keel were fashioned from huge pitch pine logs. The knees of the vessel were all cut with the natural angles of the growth from native Maine hackmatack, and fastened with locust tree-nails. A number of the Down Easters were fastened with brass or copper bolts throughout, but others used iron bolts above the ballast load line.

The bottom planking was felted and coppered up to the average salt water draft. Deck-houses were usually painted and were framed with oak and planked with white pine. Ornamentation was scarce anywhere aboard, even in the cabin, which was usually picked out with some sort of hard wood such as mahogany or teak. The bowsprits came aft into sheers; there were no fancy figureheads at all, and the ships were full-bottomed, for cargo carrying, with very little deadrise.

The bigger of the Down Easters were three-deckers, planked fore and aft. Their usual spread of canvas included three skysails, and they had short lower masts and very long topmasts. The upper topsails often had two rows of reefpoints, and the ships, as a class, rarely flew studdingsails. There were only three which carried them, and the *Paul Revere* alone carried a full suit.

Longboats aboard were carvel-built, and kept upside-down on deck. But the quarter boats, slender, classical whaleboats, were held outboard at all times, swung in the davits and ready for launching. Both rudder head and tiller were of massive oak construction, and the wheel ropes led through lignum vitae blocks. There were spittoons furnished for the wheelsmen, but, for the sailor who missed, the mates had hard, direct words. The holy stone, sand and canvas, and spotless decks were of great importance in the Down Easters.

Whitebelle is loaded with lumber until there is barely enough clearance for her booms. Such stowage practices were common with schooner operators.

These vessels were the last commercial square-riggers to be built in the United States. They remained active, mainly in the California trade, until the very serious depression of 1886 paralyzed the economy and put an end to their construction. The first of the grain carriers, the clipper bark *Greenfield,* had sailed Eastbound in 1855, and right after her came the Boston clipper *Charmer* with a full wheat cargo on a New York charter at $28 a ton. During the bumper harvest year of 1882, there were 559 ships in the trade, and they carried home from California around the Horn 1,128,031 tons of wheat and barley, and 919,898 barrels of flour.

Now that was all finished. The Maine yards went back to building schooners with three, four and five masts for the coastwise trade, and smaller, much finer two-mast craft for the fishermen who worked the waters of the Grand Banks and Georges Bank off Newfoundland. Some of the shipbuilders, lacking orders, gradually shut down and went out of business, and in Newburyport and Stonington and Mystic trade was kept alive with orders for small schooners, and sloops to be used locally by fishermen or in short-haul coastal traffic.

The last of the clippers of the Donald McKay epoch served out their time, short-rigged and sluggish, in the North Atlantic timber trade to Europe, or were cut down to coal hulks or barges. The Down Easters soon followed them, and the nation which had brought the sailing ship to the highest degree of performance in history looked forward without enthusiasm to the age of steam. Even the men who sailed the last of the square-riggers and the schooners knew that within no more than a few years they would be forced to handle power-driven craft. It was that, or stay ashore.

Steamers touched all the Maine ports, put into Nantucket and New Bedford, ran from Providence to New York on schedules just as promptly kept as the trains. Out on the Banks, the big and fast transatlantic liners were a terrible hazard for the dory-men off the fishing schooners. They were only given the chance to hear the onrush, look upward through the fog at the sharp sweep of the steel bow before the instant of final, crushing impact.

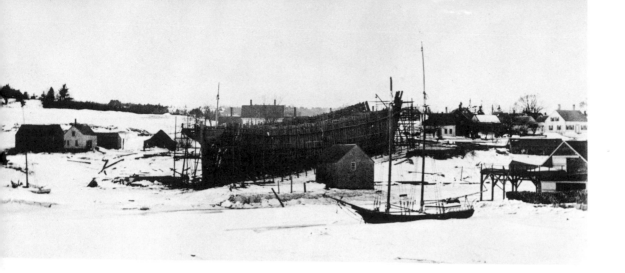

The keel of the *Baker Palmer* was laid in the early Spring of 1901, when the snow still covered the ground and the inlet waters were frozen. Through the following months the work on the frames proceeded, the masts were stepped, the shrouds rigged and the hull planked and finished.

A holiday air prevailed over Waldoboro, Maine, as the day of the launching approached. Visitors went aboard the ship, boys climbed into the rigging and little girls in floppy hats and pigtails promenaded on the main deck. The whole town came out to watch as the ship slid into the water stern first.

Flags flying, *Baker Palmer* rode easily in the calm waters of the little harbor. But years of hard usage in the coastwise trade took a heavy toll. Not quite as proud and beautiful, *Baker Palmer* limped into Boston in 1909, her bow gashed in a collision with a railroad barge.

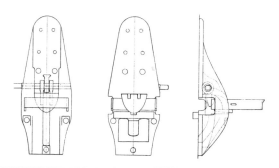

CHAPTER FIVE

Steel Hulls for Square-Riggers

. . . there were broken bones in their hands, scars on their skulls.

Industrial expansion was changing every form of life in Europe, Great Britain and the United States, and had a direct effect upon world shipping. The transportation of manufactured goods and raw materials between the continents doubled, and doubled again, and again in the second half of the nineteenth century.

Across the land, first canals and then railroads carried the huge amounts of goods. Wooden ships had shown themselves to be unsafe. Ship construction now came from the new materials in mass use, iron or steel plate, which gave much better hull protection. But increased speed was also needed. Profits would be realized just as fast as raw supplies were hauled from overseas to the factories.

But despite the lessons to be learned from what had happened to the American wooden-hulled clippers, British shipowners kept on with the same type of vessel for some years. Then, along in the 1870's, they recognized that iron plate served much better for hull construction material and they changed over to it. Their main consideration was, of course, durability, but they were also influenced by the consequent reduction of fire hazard.

Fire at sea aboard a wooden vessel that carried highly inflammable sails and tarred hemp rigging had always been one of the greatest concerns of any shipmaster. With crude and slow, hand-operated pumps, and no other fire-fighting equipment except axes and buckets, a ship might be easily consumed, and many were.

The loss of the splendidly built teakwood frigate *Cospatrick* stayed in the minds of shipowners on both sides of the Atlantic for a long time after the event. Her tragic circumstances represented an extreme case, yet showed what could take place at any time aboard another vessel.

Dalgonar, of Liverpool, England, appears almost spectral emerging from fog banks. Built in Southampton in 1892, she became a derelict in 1897.

One of the largest sailing ships ever built, the *Preussen*, of Hamburg, Germany.

Aryan, believed to be the last square-rigger of wooden construction to be built. She was launched at Phippsburg, Maine, in 1891, and was destroyed by fire at sea, December, 1918.

Cospatrick had been built in India in 1856, and was still in first class condition in 1874 when she sailed for Auckland, New Zealand from London with general cargo, 429 emigrants, and a crew of forty-four men. She was under the command of Captain John Elmslie, a veteran master, who had his wife aboard with him. *Cospatrick* had made a good run to the southward and was standing around Cape Horn in fair weather on November 17 when fire was reported.

This was at night, in the middle watch. The wind was light, Northwest, and on the quarter. "Fire!" had been cried from forward. The watch below came piling out of the focsle in their drawers and shirt tails. They were followed by the emigrants. Smoke plucked by the breeze billowed up from the fore-peak hatch. Captain Elmslie, quickly on deck, realized that the fire was in the fore-peak, and serious. The bosun kept the usual ship's stores there, which under the circumstances formed an almost explosive combination—shellack, varnish, turpentine, paint, oakum and rope.

The fire hose was connected at the main pump and led forward. *Cospatrick* was sailed off the wind. When pumping began and the fore part of the vessel was flooded, it seemed that she might be saved. But there was no fire-proof hatch that could be shut, no bulkheads that could contain the fire only to the fore-peak. Flame leaped high and streaked in the darkness along the sheets and running gear of the foremast. That finished the ship; she veered head-up into the wind.

The men handling the fire hose were driven aft by the thick, acrid masses of smoke. They were cut off from each other, and as the deck planks groaned and crackled under them with heat, the foresail caught fire. Emigrants panicked, the women screamed. Sailors could no longer hear the orders of their officers. Work was interrupted at the pump.

The fire gained furiously below. It sprang into the 'tween-decks, and then aloft

Her sails wet from a recent squall, the four-masted Swedish bark, *C.B. Pedersen,* appears bulky and clumsy. She was lost by collision in the North Atlantic on April 25, 1937.

through every hatchway, port-hole and ventilator shaft. Flame spiralled the rigging, raced swiftly along the tarred ratlines and shrouds. Then it widened out onto the yards. Sheets, braces, halyards and clewlines were next, and before they burned through and fell in charred tangles, they ignited the sails. The sails burned with wild, incandescent bursts of light; released from the gear, they dropped in great gouts of sparks upon the people crowding the main deck.

Discipline was gone. *Cospatrick's* people were seized by panic. Aflame fore and aft, there was no chance of saving her. It had taken a little over an hour for the fire to make her condition hopeless. Captain Elmslie gave the order to abandon ship.

The starboard quarter boat was lowered away and put in the water. But then, frantic with fear, emigrants piled aboard her and she was capsized. Flames licked forth at the longboat strakes when that craft was lowered from the ship, and she became useless. There were at last only two boats that got clear of the ship. They were the port and starboard lifeboats, one with forty-two persons, the other with thirty-nine aboard.

The starboard lifeboat was under the command of Henry MacDonald, the second mate. He told both boats to lie off until the ship sank. It was a slow and terrible process. *Cospatrick* took thirty-six hours to go.

Flame spread steadily aft towards the remaining people, crowded together on the poop. The foremast fell blazing, and the main, and the mizzen. When the mizzen dropped, a number of passengers on the poop were crushed to death. The rest never stopped shrieking. They gestured to Mr. MacDonald and the others in the boats— pleading for their lives.

But nothing could be done. Rescue was impossible with the boats overcrowded by weak, half-crazed men and women who sat in their night clothing, without food and water for a day and a night. Both boats lacked masts and sails, and aboard Mr. MacDonald's boat there was only one oar. He kept the craft at a safe distance from *Cospatrick*.

Her quarter galleries gave during the second day, let go with a fierce gust of heat-compressed air, a belch of smoke and flame. The people left aboard her jumped. Captain Elmslie was the last. He tossed his wife down into the sea, then leaped after her.

They drowned. The lifeboat people, unable to help them, could only sit and watch as the screaming victims begged for help. *Cospatrick* burned almost to the waterline before she sank. When she slipped beneath the waves, Mr. MacDonald gave the order, and slowly the boats moved away on the course he had reckoned.

The boats stayed together until the night of November 21, when the weather became heavy. MacDonald's survived. The other boat was never again seen. Mac-Donald rigged a sea-anchor with the painter and the oar, but lost it. Then, two days later, with pieces of wood ripped from the thwarts and floorboards, a second sea-anchor was made.

To survive the bitter competition with steamers, square-rigger men had to take chances. The *Everett C. Griggs*, renamed the *E.R. Sterling*, is loaded to the danger point. Both anchors are awash and she is taking water aboard in a fairly quiet sea.

The *Falls of Halladale,* a Glasgow-built bark of very sturdy design, was the first ship to use lifting bridges, later called cat-walks.

It held, eased the strain on the boat, and kept her up to the wind, although she was half-filled with water. During the night of November 26, just before daylight, a ship passed within fifty yards of them. They cried out with all their strength, but it was not enough, and they were not heard.

This was very hard for the survivors to take. Mr. MacDonald later testified at the inquiry that by November 27 "there were but five left—two able seamen, one ordinary, myself and one passenger. The passenger was out of his mind. All had drunk salt water. We were all dozing when the madman bit my foot and I woke up. We then saw a ship bearing down on us. She proved to be the *British Sceptre,* from Calcutta to Dundee. We were then taken on board and treated very kindly. I got very bad on board of her. I was very nigh at death's door. We were not recovered when we got to St. Helena."

While aboard *British Sceptre,* both the ordinary seaman and the passenger died. Mr. MacDonald and the two able-bodied sailors were the sole survivors out of the company of 473 persons which had left London in *Cospatrick.*

There was very little done for a long number of years afterwards to improve fire-fighting methods and enforce precautions at sea. Many ships with wooden lifeboats aboard them, would still burn like *Cospatrick* before marine underwriters, international law, and the shipowners themselves, took steps to reduce the awful hazard. But, even in the 1880's, British shipowners came to see that their crews would suffer less disability and work better if some basic safety precautions were built into the ships.

A tremendous but short-lived shipbuilding boom struck in Great Britain in 1882, shared equally between sail and steam. It was to continue until 1884, but in that interval steel hulls replaced iron, just as iron had taken the place of wood. The new ships, most of them built in the Clyde, were designed for work-a-day dependability, and not too much speed. It would take a full gale to drive one of them 300 miles in a day's run. They were cargo carriers, with nothing like clipper lines, square in the bilges, and wall-sided. The owners called them the warehouse type, and the crews said the vessels were "big, bloody well iron-box workhouses."

The type was popular, though, and remained in service until the end of British square-rigger operation. What ships survived then were sold foreign. A number of them were "four posters" in the new style, with the owners still undecided as to whether it was better to give a ship yards on all four masts or not, and whether skysails over double topgallants were worth the cost of additional hands.

Owners fully understood that interchangeable yards on fore, main and mizzen made for a great economy. That way, both riggers' and sailmakers' bills were drastically reduced. The owners also impressed upon their shipmasters the fact these ships were designed with extremely moderate sail plans. In gale weather, off Cape Horn a captain could hold onto sail as long as the gear would stand.

There was in addition, another innovation, the feature of the lifting bridges, later known as cat-walks, for the use of the crews in bad weather. Too many ships had come home short-handed. Too many men had broken arms, legs or ribs, knocked themselves senseless when swept along a main deck while trying to tend gear at a vital moment in storm. The bridges, raised above the deck, were designed to prevent this. They would allow the men to get dry-footed from forward aft in the worst of the Westerlies when it was suicidal to go down on the main deck.

The Falls Line of Glasgow, the first to install the bridges, put them in two of their ships, *Falls of Garry,* and *Falls of Halladale.* Some of the young sailors around the Russell & Company yard where the vessels were built laughed at the clumsy-looking structures. The two ships, of identical design, were 275 feet 2 inches long, with 2,026 tonnage. It was already well known that iron or steel four-masted ships of more than 250 foot length could not keep clear of heavy seas like the wooden-hulled vessels they had replaced. What was just an ordinary Cape Horn sea would rush aboard these vessels, sweep the full length of the main deck.

But old-timers had memories of Cape Horn. They remembered standing shoulder-deep in a white slash of wave crests while they hauled desperately to square a yard. Lifelines were gone from the bulwarks rails at the side. Shipmates tumbled unconscious, face-down, ready to be yanked away to death by the next wave.

Cape Horn, experienced seamen among the Russell yard group recalled, was a rough corner. There were broken bones in their hands, scars on their skulls and on shins and knee caps from Cape Horn poundings against a main deck. These steel deck bridges weren't so idiotic after all.

From forward aft, the bridges aboard *Falls of Halladale* led, first, from the focsle-head and passed the foremast to starboard, ending on the fore boat-skids on which the lifeboats rested above the deck. The next one was long, and reached to the topside of the midship house. A bridge just as long went to the half-deck topside. This pair also kept on the starboard side of the ship and stayed clear of the fife-rails and the hatches. The aftermost bridge followed the center line of the ship and crossed over the after hatch from the half-deck to the poop.

This form of cross-deck bridge construction was to be the basis of the catwalk in much later days when steam-propelled tanker ships were built. But for various reasons, most of them financial, the innovation was not adopted by many shipowners. Twilight had already darkened the future of the wind-ships that sailed under the Red Ensign of the merchant marine, and costs were kept to an absolute minimum. Most of the crews still risked their lives in the old, wide-open main deck way. That was a calculated risk for a sailor, and if a man was foolish enough to sign aboard a Cape Horn square-rigger, let him take his chances.

Falls of Halladale had her own difficult passages. She met nothing but head winds from the Tyne to the Equator during a voyage in 1893 when she carried bricks, coke and pig iron to San Francisco. Her master, Captain William Peters, took her around the north of Scotland, and when she entered the Golden Gate, she had been 187 days at sea. A mistake had been made in the ordering of slop-chest supplies, and there was an extreme shortage of tobacco. It ran out before the Equator was crossed, and after that men smoked tea and cut-up salt junk, both of which fouled their pipes, and smelled and tasted vile.

She was to make an even more unhappy run, though, when she was under the command of Captain David Wood Thomson. He took her over when she was in the Pacific grain trade to Europe, where she spent the greater part of her service. Bound for San Francisco, she sailed from Liverpool on July 25, 1903 and headed southwest across the Atlantic towards Cape Horn.

The struggle to take her around Cape Horn lasted for three bitter weeks. The big, powerful ship was swept back time and again as she tried to beat through the westerly gales into the Pacific. She lost nineteen sails, and at intervals she was hove-to without any canvas spread.

Her masts, yards and rigging received tremendous shock when sails were bent on and Captain Thomson made another try to send her westward. Rivets pulled loose in her hull plates. She began to leak badly, and both watches were turned to on the pumps. Then in the middle of a howling, miserable night, snow whipped along the wind.

The men on deck already had rope yarns secured around the cuffs of their oilskins to keep out wet, and the chin straps of their sou'westers were tight, and scarves were jammed inside collars, boots drawn high and held to their belts by straps. But moisture got in anyhow, and the men were wet, exhausted, on the verge of hysteria.

A steel hull gave greater safety to *Winterhude,* an Erikson ship.

Belle O'Neill, American schooner, flies the internationally recognized distress signal, a flag upside down.

When the snow began pelting them, Captain Thomson gave the order to stop work at the pumps. It was too wild a night to have men exposed on deck, with visibility no more than half the length of the ship.

All hands were together on the poop as a vast black wave swept aboard. There was no warning except the four-master's sudden, sidewise lurch and downward list under the enormous pressure. The wave toppled upon and submerged the entire length of the main rail. It hammered with such force that the hull resounded like a weirdly formed drum, and the topmasts bucked and swayed, yards fetched up whanging against the gear, and the pair of helmsmen could only hold onto the wheel spokes.

Then the wave was gone as the freeing ports gushed and the ship pitched and cleared her bow in answer to the helm. But Captain Thomson, looking forward from the poop into the snow blur, saw that the fore-and-aft bridges were jagged wreckage. The wave had fallen upon them, twisted and ripped the steel. It was enough. Captain Thomson turned to the men at the wheel. He told them to put up the helm. He was taking *Falls of Halladale* back, Eastward across the Atlantic to the Cape of Good Hope route, around Africa, rather than take any further risk rounding Cape Horn.

She was on very short rations when she reached port, and there was mutiny. Men wanted to get out of the ship. They hated her, and the rotten pork, the weevils and the mould in the biscuit, the pea soup that smelled like bilge, and the rusty, brackish water with which the cook made tea. But Captain Thomson was stubborn. He straightened out the crew and brought *Falls of Halladale* into San Francisco.

Her main royal mast had been lost in a storm, and so was her mizzen royal yard. Streaks of rust made her hull piebald, spread to her waterline where festoons of seaweed clung. When Captain Thomson had the pilot aboard, he explained that the ship was 238 days out of the Mersey.

But the punishment that *Falls of Halladale* took, with her heavy construction and conservative sail plan, was slight beside that suffered by some of the other Clyde-built vessels.

The full-rigged *Vincent,* owned by the New England Company, had a steel hull and was equipped with a donkey engine for windlass and capstans. But her owners maintained that "wind is cheaper than coal" and tried to compete with steamers. In the busy and congested harbor of New York, the *Vincent* relied on tugs to tow her to her dock on South Street, opposite the piers of the Bull-Insular Line in Brooklyn across the East River.

The *Vincent* carried mainly bulk cargoes, for low rates. She became a war loss in 1915 while taking baled cotton to England.

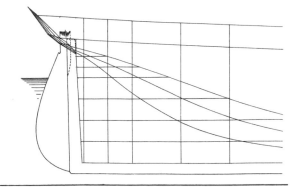

CHAPTER SIX

The Making of A Sailor

. . . she lay beam-ends under, her lower yards in the water.

THE IRON CLIPPER BEN VOIRLICH WAS built for speed. With her sharp, graceful lines, long yards and vast spread of sail she was fast. The owners, Ben Lines of Glasgow, bought her for passenger service, and safety at sea played an important part in their considerations. Yet twice the *Ben Voirlich* came close to sinking, and only exceptional luck, as her crew and the passengers aboard knew, saved her. The instincts of deepwater sailors are strange, and along the waterfront *Ben Voirlich* soon picked up the reputation of being a man-killer.

Sailor superstition proved justified on many of her voyages. Once, home-ward bound and running to westward off Cape Horn, she was struck by an enormous wave. It was on November 18, 1878. The weather was already rough. Suddenly a huge wave rose astern of the ship. It seemed to come from nowhere, without warning. There was a great roar of water. Startled, the helmsman turned around. A mountain of green was crashing down upon him. He yelled in fright and let go the wheel. The next instant the wave smashed over the stern and the *Ben Voirlich* broached, turning her side to the wind.

Nine men were swept overboard. Water cascaded through the smashed skylight, down the companionway. The cabins were gutted. Captain "Bully" Martin rushed up the companion steps, fighting his way through the onrushing water. On deck he surveyed the damage and began at once the desperate fight to save the ship.

Ben Voirlich lay beam-ends under, her lower yards in the water. Two men had been working on the foreward yardarms when the wave struck. They were swept away, one over the side to drown. The other grabbed the rail as he hurtled outboard, bumped into the chain fore-sheet and saved himself. The receding wave left him hanging head down and the next wave would certainly take him away.

But a young apprentice crawled out and grabbed the man just as the next wave hit the wallowing ship. The apprentice lost his grip and the man went over the side and disappeared. The apprentice, flung inboard, fetched up against the winch, only partly conscious. And while he lay there, the sailmaker—an old, white-bearded man—swept past him on the outward recoil of the wave. The apprentice reached out and brought the old sailor back from certain death.

Captain Martin worked for an hour to right his ship. He braced her yards around to windward three times. Then she was knocked flat again, and men dived to grope for rope ends, find pin rails and blocks to hang on. Finally the ship responded as the wheel was put up, and the wind's force upon her was lessened. She came free enough so that trysails could take her off the wind, and keep it astern.

The count the mate made showed nine men were gone. *Ben Voirlich* also lost everything movable on deck. That meant her compasses, her boats, her capstan bars and belaying pins. Her entire topgallant rail was smashed. The bulwarks had been battered away at the main deck line. She lay gaunt and ugly, still awash, clouted by the rough, chill tail of the storm. The survivors repaired the ship and finally brought her safely into port. *Ben Voirlich* was given a complete overhaul and sent back to work.

She was in trouble again eight years later, on the morning of August 6, 1885.

Ben Voirlich, a powerful iron-hulled ship of 2250 tons, sailed out of Glasgow, Scotland. Nine men were swept overboard when she was struck by an enormous wave off Cape Horn.

Captain Martin was driving her against a hard westerly gale southward of the Cape of Good Hope. He was outward-bound around Africa and wanted to make all the time possible. But a sudden squall struck and ripped the foresail right from the bolt ropes. The gale, Captain Martin realized, was fast changing into a hurricane.

Captain Martin was holding *Ben Voirlich* under fore and main lower topsails when, at about eleven o'clock in the morning, she was pooped by a sea that almost sank her. The captain was standing beside the two men at the wheel. The sea slammed down from astern, knocked him and the helmsmen off their feet.

One helmsman was pitched into the mizzen rigging, and saved himself by seizing a rope end hanging from gear on the rail. Captain Martin and the other helmsman were sent heads over feet the length of the poop deck in the wave turbulence. They landed where a chicken coop had been lashed to the bucket rail at the forward end and smashed it into fragments. Badly stunned and scratched, they still possessed strength enough to get back to the wheel.

They crawled to it over the deeply slanting deck, the spindrift knife-sharp across their eyeballs. The wheel was wrecked, and jammed in its own wreckage. Half the spokes were punched out of it; only the frame held it together. The two men worked desperately to clear away the wreckage and put helm on the ship before she turned her side to the wind. They brought *Ben Voirlich* around, but for the next twenty-four hours she was continuously swept by huge seas.

There was no way for a man to move on the main deck and live. While daylight lasted, all of the braces were led to the poop or the topsides of the deck-houses. The hurricane increased that night and ripped out of the clipper her topgallant bulwarks, her poop ladders, her harness casks, and the hen coops that had been left in their usual main deck position. Waves that were unseen and only felt in the yammering, spray-filled darkness pounded the port lifeboat to pieces. The steering compass was carried away with the binnacle in which it rested, and the standard compass went, too. Waves knocked the hand spikes out of the racks and flung them overside until there were none left aboard.

When dawn allowed him, Captain Martin had the second cabin passengers moved from their quarters to greater safety on the poop deck. It was a difficult and dangerous operation getting them onto the poop with the ladders gone, but ropes were used, and some of the people were hauled bodily to safety. The captain was afraid that the passenger deck-house would be entered by a wave, drown or kill everybody within it. He was very glad all of the ship's company were still alive. He and the mates started the necessary repairs, and found a boat compass by which *Ben Voirlich* could be steered.

Another Clydeside clipper of sturdy iron construction, the 1,250 ton *Invercargill,* was also nearly lost in similar circumstances. The helmsman let her broach in a Cape Horn gale while she was loaded with grain. She was bound from Sydney to Queenstown, and on August 27, 1904 the gale caught her.

Decks awash, the *Imperator Alexander* fights her way through the storm. It was a rough school, but working on deck under such conditions made the men expert sailors—if they survived the ordeals.

When she broached and went under to her beam ends, the shifting boards that kept the grain balanced in the holds broke, under the abrupt strain. This threw the ship further out of trim, and all of the grain settled down against her port side.

Her crew had to go below and restow the wheat, and they did not have much time. One more big sea and she might very well keep going right on down. But they took buckets and shovels and bulls-eye lanterns and crawled into the holds under a quickly lifted hatch board, and went to work.

They shoveled, carried, pushed with their hands and bodies the hundreds of tons of wheat. Chaff gagged them, made their eyes smart and tear. Seas hit the hullside, made the ship lurch deeper. Men prayed, and cursed, and then were too tired to make a sound. But eventually most of the grain was back, and the ship trimmed. The mate and the carpenter had fresh timber. They rebuilt the shifting boards. Word was passed on deck to Captain Thomas Bowling, her master.

He ordered the crew out of the holds. The hatches were tightly battened. Try-sail was bent on, and very slowly, in manouvers that took hours. *Invercargill* righted herself and stood away to her course.

The weary and dangerous Cape Horn road was known to thousands of seamen who, in the wake of Magellan, bucked the prevailing westerlies there. This old engraving by L. Haghe shows the land mass, a familiar sight to Cape Horn sailors.

But not long afterward she was again in trouble. During the morning of December 8, 1904 she began to labor heavily under the impact of a high, confused sea. The wind increased all that day, and at seven o'clock in a dull, ominous dusk, a huge sea boarded her. It broke over the port quarter and swept the entire length of the ship.

The companionway hatch on the poop deck was wrenched away from the frame. It went over the lee rail carrying away both the compasses and their binnacles. The saloon skylight was crushed, and water poured below unchecked. The cabins were flooded, then the lazarette and sail locker, and the 'tween-decks were awash.

Captain Bowling went below and found his cabin waist-deep, his charts, books and papers floating in the water. An order was passed for all hands to bail it out, and sail was rigged to cover the skylight. *Invercargill* was running wild through the night while the storm constantly increased.

Along towards dawn, the carpenter was washed out of his quarters on the main deck. He had insisted on staying there with his beloved tools, and when the wave crashed through the door, dumped him from the bunk and submerged him, he stumbled out on deck badly shocked. He knew that tons of water had entered the ship, and that her side lights had been swept away, and the screens for them. It was his impression that right now *Invercargill* was making her final lunge.

He went aft and up onto the poop. Captain Bowling was below putting the cabin

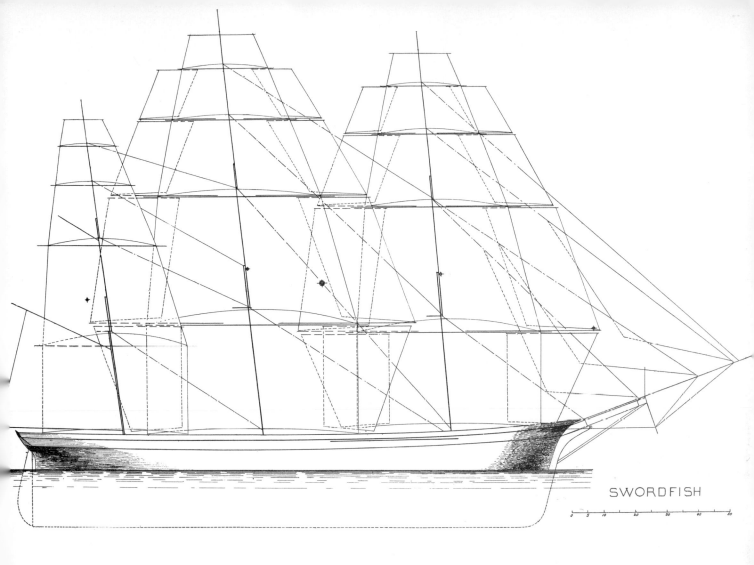

SWORDFISH

Medium clipper ship SWORDFISH

Shipbuilder William H. Webb's original plans for the remarkable ship which made one of the fastest New York to San Francisco voyages on record. The *Swordfish* proved to be a very good model for the Pacific Ocean and East India trade.

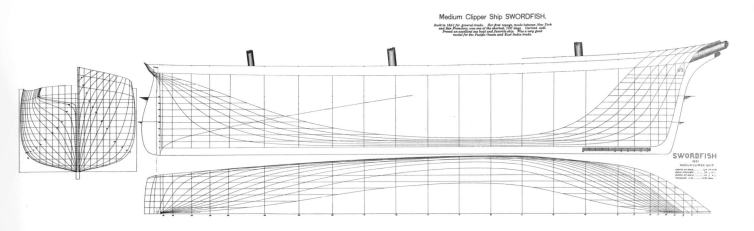

Medium Clipper Ship SWORDFISH.

SWORDFISH

MEDIUM CLIPPER SHIP

"Departure..."   Clipper ship *Rainbow*, foot of Manhattan Island   Painting by Gordon Grant

"Steamer ahead..."
Packet ship *Tiger*
Painting by J. Heard

"California clippers..."   Advertising cards, mid-nineteenth century

"Glory of sails..."
Clipper ship *Young America*
Painting by
Charles Robert Patterson

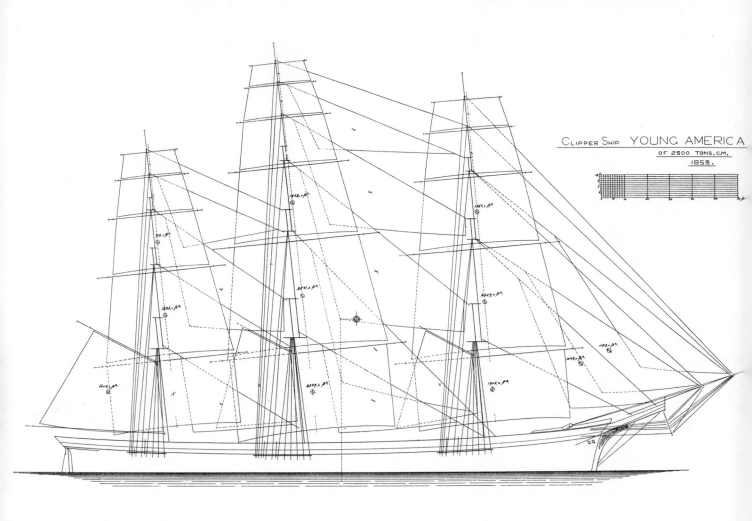

CLIPPER SHIP YOUNG AMERICA
OF 2500 TONS, C.M,
1853.

Webb ships

Original plans for two more of Webb's ships: the famous clipper *Young America* (above) and the side-wheel steamer *United States* (below). The *United States* was built for regular packet service between New York and New Orleans but was later used as a freight steamer between New York and Liverpool.

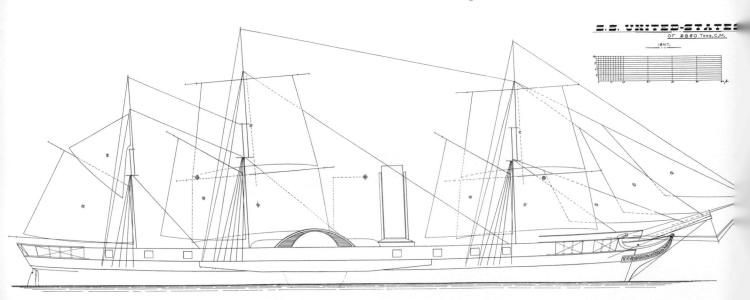

S.S. UNITED STATES
OF 2860 TONS, C.M,
1847.

in shape, the officers with him. There was nobody to countermand the carpenter when he bawled new orders at the sailor handling the wheel. The carpenter was a respected petty officer, and *Invercargill* was taking an awful beating. The sailor reversed the helm, put the wheel down and brought the clipper around into the wind.

That took out of her in immediate succession the foresail, the fore upper top-sail, fore topmast staysail, and the jib. They were followed by the main royal which was torn from its gaskets and whipped into shreds. *Invercargill* listed over with her lee fore yard arm six feet under water. The lifeboat on that side was lifted out of her davits and disappeared on a wave crest into the night.

Captain Bowling groped his way topside, quickly surveyed the damage. But there was nothing to be done until dawn. Seas slammed back and forth in fury over the length of the main deck.

Dawn showed that all along the lee rail the topgallant bulkwarks were gone. A pair of scupper ports, fashioned from thick iron plate, had been snapped from their hinges. The ends of running gear had been sucked through the apertures, chafed until they were cut ragged and useless. The ladders to the poop and to the focsle-head had been lost, and so were a number of poop stanchions. Capstan bars, hand spikes, the carpenter's tools, the contents of the bosun's locker and the paint locker also were lost.

Below, in the holds, the cargo had shifted again. Discouraged, beaten, the crew

A more recent photograph of Cape Horn verifies the accuracy of the artist, L. Haghe, who made the engraving in 1835. Although partly obscured by fog, the land is easily recognized.

The end of the schooner *Marjory Brown* on October 21, 1913 off the coast of Perth Amboy, New Jersey. She had been built not far from this spot, at Wilmington, Delaware in 1889.

moved wearily about the ship. Little could be done until the weather improved. So *Invercargill* lay with her lee rail under water for the next day and night. Then, at daylight, the men went down into the holds. For hours they worked without rest and, it seemed, in vain. In the end, Captain Bowling recognized that his ship could not be saved without dumping some of the cargo overboard. And this was done.

The weather was still thick, dangerous. But *Invercargill* was righted. Using the one battered compass left on board, Captain Bowling brought the ship on course, at least as closely as he could reckon it. *Invercargill* came into Queenstown finally, making the passage from Sydney, Australia in 113 days.

The *Priscilla* lies on the beach at Cape Hatteras, broken by the force of the storm.

There was pleasant weather and fair sailing for the *Manunui* of Sidney, Australia, when this photograph was taken. But not long after, in May, 1915, she was wrecked in a storm.

The ship was sold soon afterwards and put under the Norwegian flag. Captain Bowling retired and went to live at Christchurch, New Zealand. He had spent fifty years at sea.

By common standards his had been an eventful life. But not as seamen saw it. The dangers, the sometimes unbearable toil, the loss of life and cargo, were all part of the way of the sea. They were not yet aware that science and technology were making much of this unnecessary. Or that they themselves and their beautiful ships were rapidly becoming obsolete. Or that the ruthless needs of an expanding industrial world were more than raw courage, muscle and wind could satisfy.

Left a wreck by the fury of the storm, the bark *Alice* still has equipment worth salvaging. On the beach near Astoria, Oregon, beachcombers strip the remains.

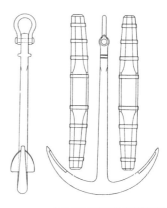

CHAPTER SEVEN

Ice, Storms and Hard Luck

. . . an unbroken wall of ice closed in.

DURING HIS 1908 EXPEDITION TO ANTARCTICA, Sir Ernest Henry Shackleton sent out a party of his men to South Georgia Island, about 1,000 miles due East of Cape Horn. While exploring the island, the men stumbled on a deeply winding, narrow bay, and what they saw floating on its waters astounded them. Surging back and forth on the waves was an almost limitless mass of flotsam wreckage, a grim record of the ships lost in the passage from the Atlantic to the Pacific around Cape Horn.

A freak of the great easterly current that flows past Cape Horn had brought the flotsam, back miles along the coast into this bay. Shackleton's men made a record of it. There were skylight benches, and teak handrails with the turk's head adornments still intact, and studdingsail poles, lifeboat rudders, and oars, a fractured companionway, and a sextant case that carried the brass plate of a famous London maker.

Piece nudged piece in a sort of endless agitation. Hatchboards bumped broken boat planks; a yard arm that trailed its gear bumped a fractured cabin table top. A sea chest lay sluggish in the current, and yet buoyant, and alongside it drifted trail boards and a light screen. The deaths of dozens of ships could be marked, but just how they had been lost, and where, were a part of the immense Cape Horn mystery.

This much was known. When an exceptionally hot summer came to the Antarctic regions, followed by protracted gales and violent seas, ice was dislodged in great quantities. Bergs that reared hundreds of feet high and weighed thousands of tons were stripped away from the mountainous ice barrier along the northern border of the South Pole continent.

They drifted in a Northeasterly direction, over thousands of miles of ocean and towards Cape Horn, which for most of the year was ice-free. The land mass at Cape Horn deflected the current directly eastward, and changed the ice drift. The bergs did not move north again until almost abreast of the Falkland Islands. They then drifted up into the warm waters of the South Atlantic and shrank to harmless size.

Three breakages from the Antarctic ice mass brought great peril to Cape Horn sailing ships in the years when records were kept. Each time huge icebergs invaded the ship routes and brought new dangers to the passage either East or West.

The first report described a vast, crescent-shaped ice island that was 60 miles wide in one direction by forty miles deep. It was sighted by twenty-one ships between December, 1854 and April, 1855. The drift of this berg was plotted between 44 degrees South latitude, 28 degrees West longitude, and 40 degrees South latitude, and 20 degrees West longitude.

The Australian auxiliary clipper *Great Britain* steamed for fifty miles along the outer edge, and stayed clear. But the Australian ship *Guiding Star* was trapped between huge ice cliffs when the breeze held fair, and yet she could not make headway against the current. She was lost with all hands. The captain of *Great Britain* and other masters who kept their vessels safe computed the height of the berg at about 300 feet.

The icebergs set loose during the second breakage in 1892–3 had a maximum height estimated at between 1,000 and 1,500 feet. Measurements were made from the waterline to the tallest peak of the berg. But even as they sighted with the sextant, the ships' officers were more concerned with leaving the ice field as quickly as possible. They needed no measurements to know that they were in imminent danger.

Captain E. H. Andrews of the full-rigged ship *Cromdale* was able to make an exceptionally detailed account in his logbook. She was a Clydesider of steel construction, built in 1891 with her sister ship *Mount Stewart*, for the Australian wool trade. Her tonnage was 1,903 and her overall length 271 feet 6 inches; she was still a new ship, in fine condition, when she ran into the ice field off the Horn.

She had left Sydney homeward-bound on March 1, 1892 and rounded the Horn on March 30 without seeing ice. Her position at midnight on April 1, 1892 was 56 degrees South latitude, 58 degrees 32 minutes West longitude. The temperature was 37.5 degrees. At first there was no sign of ice, although off to the southward Captain Andrews saw a suspicious glare along the horizon.

A sharp lookout was maintained, and at four o'clock, with the first dawn light, a big berg was reported bearing dead ahead. *Cromdale* was hauled around and saved. Then, half an hour later, with visibility extended, several bergs were seen to windward. Captain Andrews was steering Northeast, the wind out of the Northwest, and his ship's speed about nine knots.

Full realization of the danger came with the dawn. The entire horizon to windward was filled by a gigantic mass of icebergs. Behind the ship another wall of ice had

Typical of transition vessels, the steamer bark *Scotia* was built at Drammen, Norway in 1872 and used in Arctic explorations. She was destroyed by fire in 1916.

The beautifully kept, full-rigged British ship *Cromdale* still clings to the traditional false gun ports painted along her waist. She survived the dangerous ice fields off Cape Horn only to be wrecked on her home coast.

The three-masted schooner, *Leona and Marion*, one of the last of her kind, was built in 1920. She foundered off Nova Scotia on February 6, 1938.

closed in. Scintillant in the sunlight, it reared in an unbroken line. Other bergs, some large, some small drifted to leeward of the *Cromdale*.

Captain Andrews called all hands. He reduced sail, but kept a speed of seven knots. The men were given coffee and their breakfast, and stayed on deck at their stations. They waited silently as the walls of ice merged ahead of them.

At seven-thirty Captain Andrews sent the chief mate aloft with binoculars to find a passage ahead through the ice-field. From the main topgallant yard the mate observed the bergs and finally hailed the captain to inform him no passage existed ahead. *Cromdale* was sailing within an ever-closing stretch of water, the walls of the icebergs slowly converging. And each of the bergs was large enough to sink the ship. The technical term for *Cromdale's* danger was "embayed."

Unable to sail ahead, Captain Andrews tried to get out of the bay while he still had time. He tacked the ship and tried to get into open water. Some of the bergs were so close that the *Cromdale* scraped its hull against them. The yardarms were swung to prevent them from being smashed against the ice cliffs which rose 300 feet upward, sheer, smooth, and cut straight. Great splatters of wind-driven spray leaped over their southerly sides, and showed the wind force sweeping from there.

Captain Andrews kept on tacking ship in the space that was left. He had gained some headway, believed he might have a chance to haul clear when around eleven o'clock the wind veered. It changed with every squall that rushed in over the bergs, and *Cromdale* was drawn close to the southern barrier. There did not seem to be any hope for her, and all hands knew how quickly they would die, either in the water or upon the shoulder of some berg.

Along about eleven-thirty in the morning, though, the wind shifted to Southwest with a strong squall. That was what Captain Andrews wanted. He sailed *Cromdale* to the Northwest, and while she made good the course, he had a good look at some of the bergs. The largest of them was about 1,000 feet high and in the shape of an anvil. Back in the bay, at least fifty had been black, and straight from the waterline to their pinnacles. By two o'clock in the afternoon Captain Andrews could look astern from open water. *Cromdale* held her Northwest course and was beyond the northern arm of the horseshoe-shaped mass. It reached from one side of the bow around to as far as he could see astern.

He ended his logbook entry:

"I have frequently seen ice down south, but never anything like even the smaller bergs in this group."

A number of other ships in the Australian wool fleet reported huge masses of ice off the Horn that year. A stupendous barrier stretched from approximately 37 degrees West longitude to 25 degrees West, along the parallel of 45 degrees South latitude. The three-mast bark *Strathdon* owned by the Aberdeen White Star Line entered the field on March 18 at 45 degrees South latitude and 25 degrees West longitude. Then, for over a month, until May 21, she tried to find a way through, and kept her hands occupied at short-tack drill while she dodged icebergs.

The schooner *Governor Ames* was built in Waldoboro, Maine, in 1888, and wrecked off Cape Hatteras on December 13, 1909. Only one member of her crew was saved, the rest went down with the ship.

The bark *Maria Borges,* built in 1884 by J. Reed and Co. of Port Glasgow, lasted until March 27,

The captain of the *Strathdon* estimated some of the bergs as 1,000 feet in height, and others around 800 feet. His report was confirmed by estimates made by other ships that came in contact with the field, among them *Loch Eck, Curzon, Liverpool,* and *County of Edinburgh.* Then, in the following year of 1893, even greater heights were reported.

Turakina said that in 51 degrees South latitude and 47 degrees West longitude she had avoided a berg 1,200 high. The famous clipper *Cutty Sark* reported a height of 1,000 feet at a position a bit further North, and *Brier Holme* and *Charles Racine* gave the same 1,000 foot calculations for bergs they found in the area. They had all threaded their way through with immense difficulty, and their masters were quick to praise themselves when they got home. But no vessels were lost during the 1892–3 period due mainly to fine seamanship, and the boasting was justified.

The next great test came in 1908 when a new mass of ice broke away from the Antarctic ice field. Ships worked their way through the field under the most dangerous circumstances. *Ben Voirlich* was one of the vessels that was nearly lost. She collided with a berg, suffered injury to her jibboom and bowsprit before she could stand clear on a safe course.

Over the years, of the ships threatened by the Cape Horn ice, *Cromdale* had been in the worst danger—and came through safely. But she seemed to have spent all her good luck there. It was her fate, ironically, to be lost on her own home coast,

1922. She sank on an even keel off Newport News, Virginia, with her topmasts and yards standing.

and because of a mistake that was not of her own making. The square-rigger was given a wrong position by a steamer she met in fog off Lizard Rock at the southern end of England. Captain Arthur, the master of *Cromdale,* trusted the steamer captain's reckoning, and piled up his vessel at the foot of Lizard Light.

Cromdale had come around from Taltal, a small port on the west coast of South America, on a slow passage of 120 days, bound for Falmouth, England. She was off Lizard Rock when the fog thinned, sighted the steamer, and asked for a position. The steamer master told Captain Arthur he was off course and to haul two points to the northward.

Captain Arthur altered course, but also took the precaution of shortening sail. The weather was again very thick on the night of May 23, and he knew that he was somewhere close in to the coast, although he had no reliable bearings. Then the vast beam of Lizard Light was seen ahead, so powerful and so high that it could not be mistaken. *Cromdale,* unless she was hauled off fast, would strike right at the foot of the cliff.

All hands were called to stations. But before *Cromdale* could come about she fetched up hard and badly holed herself. Water started pouring into her lower holds. She was carrying at the time her main lower topgallant sail, lower topsails and two jibs. The wind was light, but enough to tear the bottom out of her, and Captain Arthur knew that she was finished.

An artist's visualization of a rescue performed by a shore-based lifeboat. The saving of the *Cromdale's* crew was very similar to this.

The curious gather to watch rescue operations as the wreckage of the schooner *Augustus Hunt* is washed ashore on the beach at Quogue, New York, January 21, 1904.

The wreckage of the schooner *Dora A. Baker* became a fixture at Long Branch, New Jersey. The scene was sketched for "Harper's Weekly" in 1867 by Charles Parsons.

The boats were ordered into the water. Mrs. Arthur was aboard and she stayed beside her husband, and was with him the last to abandon ship. The boats were rowed away into the smooth waters farther offshore and from there the ship's company of twenty-eight watched *Cromdale* die. The ship rested on the rocks, refusing to settle down, and after a while the crew made plans to return aboard to save their personal possessions.

From up on the Lizard cliff shouts hailed the survivors. Men were climbing part way down the cliff. *Cromdale,* when she beached, made such a noise that it had roused the men at the Lloyd's signal station.

Now they called down, anxious to help. They could see *Cromdale* where she lay, and the director of the signal station fired off the two-rocket distress signal. That brought the local lifeboats. They took Mrs. Arthur and the crew aboard and led the ship's boats off on painters. Captain Arthur, however, was determined to save what he could from the ship. He asked for volunteers and got them quickly. The Lizard lifeboat took them out to the wreck.

The *Cromdale* was beginning to settle when they climbed aboard. An able-bodied sailor named Nightingale went into the focsle and brought up the men's sea-bags and chests. Others of the volunteers passed these aft quickly and into the Lizard boat. In the end, all that was lost was a cash box that belonged to a Swedish sailor. But it contained his life's savings, £50.

Nightingale then pressed his luck and entered the main cabin. The water was up to his neck as he went down the companionway ladder. But he groped around, found the ship's papers and took them on deck to Captain Arthur. *Cromdale* settled abruptly as the rocks ripped the bottom from her. The main deck was awash, and the men leaped for the rigging.

The Lizard boat came alongside, took them off, put them ashore with Mrs. Arthur and the rest of their shipmates. Captain Arthur waited for dawn to see what could be done for his ship. But she was in the clasp of the long, unremitting Atlantic swells. They broke her up, and sank her.

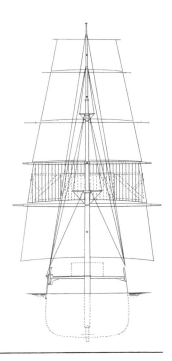

CHAPTER EIGHT

Destruction In Dead Calm

. . . put me on an island where the girls are few.

THE BELIEF IN THE SAILING ABILITIES and in the economic worth of wind-driven ships died hard. There were men in Great Britain, even as late as 1900, who persisted with their operation of square-rigged vessels, and were not at all ready to admit that steampower had replaced sail. They brandished their cost sheets as proof of their argument, and cited what was being done by the Laeisz Line of Hamburg, Germany, and by many Norwegians and Finns.

Fire at sea was certainly a problem, the old-time shipowners admitted. The horror of the *Cospatrick* disaster could not be easily forgotten. But there was a solution for that. Vessels were being built out of iron, or even steel. Putting auxiliary motors, or steam engines, into ships was another matter. It was sheer, wasteful stupidity, old-line shipowners insisted. Think of the coal that was burned up during the course of a long voyage, and of the profit-making cargo space that was taken up by the coal bunkers. And steamships? Sail-ship owners could express their opinion only in old-fashioned, salty language.

Still, the sailing ships that were sent to sea without auxiliary motors were becalmed for weeks at a time while consignees waited for cargo. The ships drifted helplessly while they waited for a breeze in regions of strong currents. And sometimes they drifted into disaster. Steampower could have saved them, but they relied on the fickle, uncertain forces of the wind.

Big cargo carrier *Ruth E. Merrill* being towed into harbor. Eventually sailing ships relied almost entirely on steam-powered tugs in busy harbors.

The history of the United Fruit Company demonstrates the dramatic change from sail to steam ships. The *Jesse H. Freeman* commissioned in 1883, was equipped with an auxiliary coal-burning steam engine but relied mainly on her sails.

The great, splendidly built British square-riggers disappeared one by one. They were nearly gone in 1900 from the Cape Horn run, and the owners did not replace them. The opening of the Suez Canal in 1869 and then the establishment of coaling stations for steamers along the major sea routes had speeded the end. Sail ships during the 1900–1910 period could no longer compete for premium cargo and were limited to cheap, bulk haul work. Their owners laid them up one by one, or took the masts out and made them into scows, or sold them for scrap.

Cape Horn, always a lonely, desolate region, became a deserted stretch of water for weeks at a time. Now, if disaster came there, a ship's crew saved itself, or was lost. The men of the *Deccan* learned that during her last voyage. She was a full-rigged, three-mast ship from Liverpool and sent in August, 1909, around the Horn with a cargo of coal. Her loading port was Port Talbot, Wales, her port of call Tocopilla, on the West Coast of South America.

Early in the voyage, her master, a man named Parnell, fell seriously ill, and nothing that the chief mate, the second mate and the steward could find in the "Shipmasters' Medical and Surgical Guide" helped his condition. Then the inevitable rumor-monger in the focsle spread the story, later verified, that on the previous voyage two men had been killed aboard. This had happened on the West Coast during a mutiny; the men were killed when they were thrown down into the hold. The crew soon came to call her a hard luck ship.

It was the Captain's fault, the crew believed. Once he was out of her, their luck would be all right again. But *Deccan* was 84 days at sea before she reached Port Stanley in the Falkland Islands. The captain, about to die, was put aboard the mail ship for home, and at the cable orders of the owners the chief mate was appointed master. His name was Rowlands. Although under thirty, he was a very capable officer and held an extra-master's certificate.

In 1885 the wooden hulled *Lorenzo Dow Jones* was built in Bath, Maine. Because propulsion came mainly from the coal-fed steam engine, the sails became relatively unimportant. *Admiral Dewey* (right), built in Philadelphia in 1898, and one of four similar Admiral ships, carried 35,000 bunches of bananas. Her speed of better than 14 knots was almost twice that of the *Jesse H. Freeman*.

Most of the crew were Welshmen, and superstitious. They liked Rowlands' appointment, but they were dispirited by the fact that three days after the ship had reached port, one of the apprentice seamen died of mysterious causes. Then the new chief mate, whose name was Thomas, came aboard. His former ship was *Great Britain* and she had burned here in the harbor. The crew didn't like that, believed it meant bad luck. They added new forebodings when a new apprentice came aboard to replace the one who had died.

When *Deccan* caught fire as she was being towed out of the harbor by her tug the focsle hands failed to be surprised; it only verified their worst fears. But Captain Rowlands acted promptly and located the source of the fire in the sail locker. He kept the tug on the towline while a bucket brigade was formed, water passed below until the smouldering sails were doused. With the sailmaker at work repairing the damage, he told the tug to cast off, and headed for Cape Horn.

Deccan had the usual bitter struggle with the westerly gales off Tierra del Fuego. She took what she could from the offshore winds, and beat up past Diego Ramirez into the Pacific. She was making good time, the focsle skeptics admitted. Three weeks after she had left the Falklands, on December 6, 1909, she was abreast of Cape Tate, more than 300 miles Northwest of the Horn.

But the pessimists said, wait. *Deccan* was still a long way from Tocopilla. A man never knew what was going to happen in these treacherous waters.

During the afternoon of December 6, the wind which had blown strong and steady from the land all morning, suddenly fell. There was flat calm. *Deccan* began to drift inshore, thrust by the powerful Easterly current. Long, hard swells put up breakers on the rocky beach. Captain Rowlands studied that and then told the mate to bend on all canvas.

The sails hung slatting in the gear with the roll of the dark-backed swells. The men stood by the braces, silent, watching their ship drift shoreward. They waited for *Deccan* to strike. There was no hope for her without a stiff offshore breeze.

Captain Rowlands gave the order for the boats to be swung outboard. It was being obeyed when *Deccan* grounded. Her steel hull shuddered and screeched as she lunged onto the rocks, pitched, drove a bit more and stopped. Water began filling her holds through the ripped bottom plates. Swung by the current and the inflow of water, she listed over on her bilge and began to pound. The blows were massive, and deadly. She could not last long and was about to lose her masts.

The captain and the chief mate stayed aboard while the two lifeboats were launched and drew away from the ship. Then they jumped from her, and behind them, plummeting, the masts went over the side in vast smothers of spray. Captain Rowlands and Chief Mate Thomas swam to a boat and were taken aboard. The life boats then pulled to seaward to keep clear of the rock that had finished *Deccan,* and to stay out of the surf. But they rested on their oars long enough to take a last look at the ship.

Pilot boards the *Brynhilda* as she approaches the entrance to New York harbor. Anchored in the Narrows between Staten Island and Brooklyn she waited days, sometimes weeks, for her turn to be towed to a pier. There were still enough bulk-carrying sail ships in use to crowd many docks. *Brynhilda* finally went to the shipbreakers in 1923.

Another Glasgow-built ship, the bark *Killeena*, served her owners from 1875 until she was dismantled in 1922. The photograph emphasizes the helplessness of a sail vessel without wind.

Deccan was gone twenty minutes after she struck. There was a little wreckage to mark the grave and that was all. The men sat grim-faced at the oars. Some of them had sailed this coast before and knew of the dangers ashore. The rest gazed at the snow-crested range of mountains that towered beyond the thin, barren strip of beach. One man ventured to speak.

"Even if we land here," he said, "where do we go, sir?"

Captain Rowlands ignored the question. He said, "We must find a place to lay our heads before dark."

But it took hours of gruelling, unbroken pulling at the oars before they reached shore.

Cape Tate and the coast to the southward could not be approached because of the surf. The captain put the boats on a northerly course, and the twenty-seven men rowed hard, with all the energy they owned. The sea was still calm. They knew what would happen if a wind picked up and caught them offshore at night.

Both boats landed on a small, sandy piece of beach just before dusk. Captain Rowlands identified the place as being on the southern shore of Desolation Island, some miles north of where *Deccan* had been lost. The sails were taken from the boats and set up as tents. He divided the company into two groups, with himself, the chief, the second mate and the apprentices in one tent, the crew in the other.

The stores taken from the ship consisted of 60 pounds of canned meat and two bags of biscuit. The biscuits were sodden from being left on the floorboards of the badly leaking boats. Captain Rowlands decided to wait until dawn before he issued rations, and told the men to make a fire. There were axes, kerosene and hermetically sealed matches in the boats, and a sailor supplied his cap lining for tinder after a tree had been chopped.

The fire blazed high with a sprinkling of kerosene and the men were very grateful for it. Wind had picked up, and howled, and rain accompanied it. The sails that served as tents gave small protection; the best the company could do was shoulder around the fire. They were dressed in the sodden oilskins or the dungarees they had worn when fighting to save *Deccan*. Some of the old-timers who shivered so hard that they were unable to explain themselves, went down to the beach and dunked head to feet in the surf. The reason for that, their focsle-mates told the uninitiated, was to keep from getting pneumonia. Salt water was a cure for colds, they believed.

It was a miserable night, and just as wet and windy at daybreak. Captain Rowlands issued a biscuit to each man and then asked approval to stop drawing upon their meager supplies. There were fresh water streams close by on the island, and limpets and mussels for food. The men soberly agreed. Captain Rowlands talked the situation over with his mates, then suggested they attempt to march across the mountain range. Beyond the mountains that hemmed them in on the narrow coast they would probably find some native habitation.

The shivering men took up his suggestion enthusiastically. The boats were careened high up on the beach, the tents struck, and packs of equal weight made after a meal of mussels. Soon after midday, in the pelting rain, they shuffled off towards the 3,000 foot high mountains.

Terrain was very rough on the mountain-side. Feet softened by hours of immersion in salt water rubbed bloody in thick boots. The apprentices tried to sing, but that did not last long. When Captain Rowlands gave the order for a halt, the men threw themselves down and slept sprawled out in the wind and the rain.

Captain Rowlands soon realized the difficulties ahead, took his men back down the mountainside to the former camp. They would have perished up there. A fire was started, and the tents pitched again; the weary men enjoyed a bit of warmth.

Rowlands asked his men if they were willing to make a try at sailing the boats along the coast. All hands agreed, and, at dawn, the clumsy boats were run offshore through the surf. But the wind was wrong. They could not sail or row against it. Hours later they were forced to land miles to the southward of their former camp site. The talk that night was of disaster, doom, and death. Old stories about Desolation Island, once heard in dockside saloons, were repeated, and dour Welsh predictions made about the future of *Deccan*'s men.

Captain Rowlands listened and recognized what must be done at dawn. He mustered the entire company, told them that they were going to march with him across the mountain range. It was, he said bluntly, the one hope they had left. There was no dissension. The men struck camp almost silently, and followed him towards the mountains.

But nearly all of them were incapable of the effort. They sagged and fell, and when helped up by their mates, fell again, and lay motionless. Boots were cut apart on the rocks; knees, elbows were raw. Men wept, and were unaware they made the sound. The captain led them back to the camp at the cove. Their situation seemed hopeless.

But on the seventh day Rowlands gathered the strongest men. He would make

another attempt, he told them, and they were to go with him. The sick and the weak were to stay in the charge of Mr. Thomas, and wait. He would return with the help that was sure to be found on the other side of the mountains.

The men he had chosen arranged their packs, lashed the soles of their boots to the uppers. Those who stayed and those who were to go shook hands and wished each other luck. Mr. Thomas went a short way with Captain Rowlands, watched the party climb up into the mountain snow, and finally disappear from sight.

Mr. Thomas heard a rifle shot four days later. He looked around to seaward and saw a boat at the water's edge. Captain Rowlands was wading ashore, and with him were three Chileans. They carried biscuit, and canned meat, and a bucket of tea that steamed and brought even the sick men to their feet.

They had crossed the mountains and reached the Magellan Strait, Captain Rowlands told his men. There they had been sighted by the crew of a Chilean sealing cutter that lay anchored close to the beach. She was on her last expedition of the year and bound back to her base at Punta Arenas. Luck was finally with the *Deccan* men. The cutter was out of sight, beyond the nearest headland, but she was standing by to take all hands to Punta Arenas.

The British consul hurried down to the cutter on December 20, 1909 when she reached the little Chilean port off the Strait of Magellan. He had brought a doctor with him, and the sick were given the best possible care. But ten of the men died.

The survivors returned to Liverpool on January 28, 1910, where the Shipwrecked Mariners' Society took charge of them, gave them enough money to get home. One of those men, recalling the experience years afterwards, said that at the time there was a popular song in England that went, "Put me on an island where the girls are few."

"When *Deccan* was outward-bound," he said, "we often used to sing that song."

Schooners still carried a good deal of bulk cargo along the American coasts after World War I. But, like the five-masted *Frank M. Deering,* they lasted a few years longer only because of the help from tugs in harbor waters. Usually they picked up cargo in remote outports along rugged, little-known coasts. In the clutch of strong tides, many suffered the fate of the *General Grant* (below), here sketched by an artist.

Aboard the *Annie C. Ross* the towline was brought up by hand. A steam donkey engine was used to raise the sails, but muscle power still carried much of the work-load. A man hauled at heavy gear until he was glaze-eyed with fatigue, and then had to go aloft to work on the rigging. Sailors cursed the American schooners and called them "workhouses" and worse.

Once the *Annie C. Ross* is under way, a lookout is sent up while the rest of the crew stumbles below. Supper was highly welcomed when hustled forward from the galley. With the weather clear, the wind aft and the sails set wing-and-wing, the helmsman had an easy trick at the wheel.

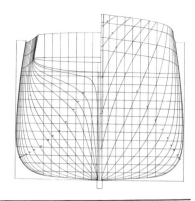

CHAPTER NINE

Masters and Men

. . . a hungry man will sail in anything that floats.

As the end of commercial usefulness of the big sailing ships came closer, shipowners were beset by too many greater difficulties to worry much about manpower problems. There were always enough sailors on the waterfront. Sometimes the men could not speak the language of the country in whose vessels they served, and often they deserted the ship at the first port of call. Shipowners and masters accepted this philosophically. In a trade that had shrunk to a quarter of its size from 1880 to 1900, crew replacements were a minor consideration.

It was a time of great turmoil and change among the men who went to sea. Former traditions were disappearing; new traditions were only beginning to arise. A footloose able-bodied sailor might make a voyage in the *Great Eastern,* the mammoth paddle-wheel steamer of British construction. She was equipped with a 24-foot propeller and six masts to carry sail. But rarely were the sails used, and few were the sailors who cared. The *Great Eastern* displaced 22,500 tons; her length was 693 feet, and she had a beam of 120 feet. She was almost fantastically bigger than any other contemporary vessel. This meant little to her crew. She was just another ship to them.

The same sailor would leave the steamship *Great Eastern* at any port that struck his fancy, then ship out aboard a crude sail tanker like the *Charles.*

One of the first of the tanker ships, *Charles* was square-rigged and built expressly for the oil trade. She had a capacity of 59 tanks, and they leaked. Shipowners and insurance people had no faith in steamers as carriers of inflammable oil. A natural fire hazard, they said. And they were wrong. Eventually the sail ship *Charles,* like many of the sail tankers, burned at sea, with heavy loss of life.

Crews were still found for the rest along Lime Street in Liverpool, and the East India Dock Road in London, South and Cherry Streets in New York, and around Scollay Square in Boston. The shipowners believed if a man were hungry enough, he would go to sea in anything that floated. The discharge books of the 1880–1900 period showed that sailors shipped out with no particular type of vessel in mind.

They had no national preference, except that generally British seamen stayed away from American ships, and the other way around. Because of the great language barrier, Americans rarely signed articles aboard Scandinavian ships. But, otherwise, their choice was completely free. They were not company men. There was no seniority system for them, and no pension. The only attractions for a certain ship would be if she were known as a good-feeder, and if the captain and the chief mate did not hold the reputation for being "bully boys" and harsh in their treatment of the crew.

Men lost their sense of nationality after a few years in the focsles of the deepwater ships. They talked a polyglot language, most of it English, but with Spanish, Scandinavian and Malaysian words in it. The bosun was often called *tuan;* the topgallant sail was known as the *bram;* a man would tell his watchmate to move *muy rapido.*

This kind of life fostered eccentric characteristics. Some of the men, among them the older sailors, would not leave a ship when she was alongside the dock in port. They were divorced from shore. The ship was home. They knew little but the working of her. The future was death in a storm, or a vague, bleak last few years in a seamen's boarding-house on the money that had been saved. The younger men when they went ashore very seldom left the dockside area. They spent their money in saloons that catered to sailors and were almost identical around the world. The majority of them could not read or write; their severance from their families was complete. Their single, fierce pride was the ability to perform a ship's work quickly, and with great skill.

A man who could read was given respect in a focsle. He deciphered old letters, and newspapers, recited the Board of Trade regulations so that the other men might memorize them. Then there were amateur doctors, and those who admitted to being broken-down gentlemen and former chief mates, and outright crackpots who should never have been allowed to come aboard. One Cape Horn ship of the period carried in her focsle a shaggy-headed sailor who was soon given the nickname of Paraffin. It was his habit to eat a mouthful of the stuff every morning before going out on deck. That, he said, kept out the cold.

Paraffin lasted around the Horn, but was in pretty poor shape when the ship reached San Francisco. He was taken to the hospital for extensive overhaul.

"His bilges was kinda clogged," a shipmate said of him.

Eccentric behavior was, however, not confined to the crew. Masters felt the tremendous strain of their responsibilities, and suffered keenly from the isolation that command enforced upon them. The master of the fine, full-rigged British ship *Tamar* coming down the Elbe River out of Hamburg, bound for Seattle, appeared on deck

Great Eastern, the strangest combination of steam and sail ever introduced into one hull, lies at anchor in a Newfoundland harbor. In the 1870's she was used to lay cable lines across the Atlantic.

staggering drunk, a pistol in his hand. This was in narrow Channel waters. Without warning he fired a shot at the able seaman at the wheel.

The bullet missed, and the second mate had time to get between the sailor and the captain. But the captain brandished the pistol and ordered the course changed to the southward. When the chief mate came on deck, he protested, and followed the captain into the chart-house. It was now almost dark; the mate could see the lighthouse looming, over the port bow.

Still the captain insisted that the course was right, and to prove it, tore up the lighthouse guide and the other navigation books. He told the mate that the course was not to be changed. As master, he held full responsibility for the ship. *Tamar* was now heading straight for the rocks within two miles of her.

The mate made a sudden movement and the captain fired at him. He missed, and the mate jumped him, and aided by the second officer, overpowered the captain. *Tamar* was braced around and set on a new course. The captain was handcuffed and

The *Mariposa* of Liverpool, England unloading her cargo at San Francisco in 1880. She had been built in 1874.

A fine example of the Hermaphrodite type ship, believed to be the *Margaret L. Vinnen*.

confined, and the ship taken into Plymouth, where the owners turned over the case to the court.

Perhaps even more peculiar behavior was exhibited by Captain William McGowan, master of the Scottish iron-hulled clipper *Benvenue*. He was known as "Mad" McGowan for the way he held on to sail in a storm when other masters displayed far more caution. Yet what appeared as his maddest prank took place in Glasgow when his ship was tied up alongside the dock and, according to witnesses, he was sober. He hung a large sign in the rigging.

"No Irish Need Apply."

The ship was docked in the notorious Govan area of the city. It was crowded with Irish people who had been driven to Scotland by severe famines at home. The men sought work in the Clydeside shipyards and ships, and were sharply disliked by their Scottish neighbors. Captain McGowan's sign brought an instant barrage of refuse, dead cats and public-house crockery. Then a number of strapping Irishmen,

Stubby-bowed *Deerhill* loading at a cargo-littered dockside. Horse-drawn drays (left) and the steam donkey engine (right) were a common sight on the docks.

the pick of their kind in the port, boarded *Benvenue* and demanded work as sailors.

Captain McGowan hired enough to fill the starboard watch, half of the crew. For the other half, the port watch, he hired men just as big and strong. All of them were American, sailors who had learned their trade in the Cape Horn clippers. They were Negroes, nearly all from Carroll County in Virginia, where seagoing had been a tradition for centuries.

Irishmen who already smarted from underprivilege became furiously angry and jealous of their Negro shipmates. There was extreme competition on deck and aloft when *Benvenue* put to sea. Fights between men of the two watches inevitably followed; both sides nursed their wounds, and after a while the friction disappeared. The watches worked together amiably and well throughout the rest of the voyage.

But "Mad" McGowan was far from mad. Nor was he playing some grim racial joke. The shrewd Scotsman had simply schemed up a way of getting himself just about the best crew that ever sailed a ship. The national and racial rivalry gave him the chance to squeeze more hard work out of both watches than any master had ever succeeded in getting from his men.

Yet this same McGowan showed more concern for the welfare of his crew than many another master. His ships invariably were good feeders and the focsle was as comfortable as could be gotten under the conditions then prevailing.

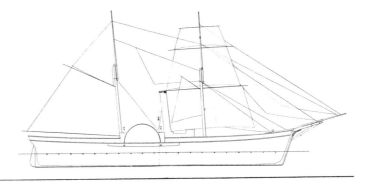

CHAPTER TEN

Sailor Men and Steamer Stiffs

. . . no more freeboard than a frying pan.

It HAD BEEN EASY TO FIND skilled men for American ships before the Civil War. Then came the decline of the clipper and the westward expansion. Wages fell in the great ports of the East. More and more of the jobs aboard sailing ships were filled by foreign seamen. Almost imperceptibly the great seagoing tradition was vanishing from the old coastal communities.

There was still a career in sail for British and European young men. Their countries considered square-rigger training important for future officers, either in the navy or in the merchant marine. But the American government completely disregarded this practice, and American crews for whalers and deepwater ships became increasingly difficult to find. Men were willing to work in the fishing schooners, and the coastwise vessels. But not much appeal was left for the Cape Horn run, or for an absence from home of two or three years.

When the Civil War broke out, the men called into the United States Navy served mainly in steam-propelled vessels, or frigates and sloops-of-war that were moved by both steam and sail. A group of about 100 British officers, a number of them on half-pay leave from the Royal Navy, picked up steamer knowledge at the same time. They ran the blockade between the Bahamas and the Confederate-held ports on the Atlantic coast and made huge pay-offs from the traffic.

When the war ended, a new generation of American seamen had been created. The sailing ship men called them "steamer stiffs," but the men who worked in the steam-driven vessels, deck officers and engineers, were not greatly concerned. They could see the future, and sail had small part in it. They had, further, inherited the tradition of the first steamer men who, particularly in the Port of New York, were a hardy and stubborn breed.

In the preceding decades, small steamers had been making steady inroads into commercial shipping. At first their influence was felt only in the river trade, then gradually it spread along coastal waterways. Even while clipper ships gloried in their superiority, steamers were taking over a considerable amount of cargo and passenger transportation.

The early American steamers of the 1820–30–40 era represented enormous danger for their crews. They carried such names as *Dreadnought,* and rightly so. A description of a pioneer steam craft made even sailing ship men wince. They gathered in the bars along New York's South Street and listened grimly as steamer men described how close the water came to the deck line.

"She has no more freeboard than a frying pan!"

The comparison of a steamer to a floating frying pan was accurate enough. Typical dimensions of the vessels built to run the harbor, the Hudson River and Long Island Sound were frightening: 112-foot length over all, 24-foot beam and only a 4-foot draft. The bow was round, the stern square, and she was made not of iron but of live-oak. The paddle wheels were very far forward, the boiler back behind the engine. The shaft worked like a see-saw across the steeple-like engine, and often jammed dead center. Then it took all hands working with iron bars to pry it into operation again.

The cabin was aft. Just forward of it, projecting three feet above the deck, was the pure copper boiler. The pilot-house was up on a gallows frame over the fore deck, leaving space below it for fire wood.

PAINTING BY SAMUEL WALTERS

The United States Mail steamship *Atlantic* sailing up the Mersey River after crossing the Atlantic, New York to Liverpool, in 13 days.

The sail-and-steam *Western Metropolis* used an engine of the "walking beam" type. Note the foremast rising through the deckhead of her wheelhouse..

The usual signal equipment between the pilot-house and the engineer was a jingle bell. When that was rung, it meant "Ahead." When need was found to back the vessel, the big ship's bell on the pilot-house was struck. "Full Ahead" and "Full Astern" were signalled by stamping on the pilot-house floor, and the engineer was sure to hear, despite the engine sounds; he stood directly underneath the pilot-house.

Crank shafts were made of cast iron, and the same material was used for all other working parts. Boiler pressure was maintained at 21 pounds. When under way, the engine vibration shook the safety valve so much it had to be tied down. But if it was left tied down too long, excess steam pressure would blow out the wall of the boiler.

A man who worked aboard such craft might at any moment be blown up by boiler failure, beheaded by a piece of fractured engine machinery, rammed and drowned by competitors in sailing vessels or other steamers, and beaten senseless on the dock by various factions of the opposition.

Deliberate rammings off the New York's Battery and along the Hudson and East Rivers were daily occurrences. A good many were avoided only because the rammers feared the boiler explosion would sink their own craft. And when steamer competition stiffened, collisions became more frequent and often serious, with major injury to passengers, crews and vessels. One steamer captain, flipping over the wheel so that his vessel slammed bow-on into another, let out a joyous yell at the moment of impact: "There she goes, right into the goddamn' ladies' cabin!"

PAINTING BY CHARLES ROB[...]

South Street in the Port of New York in 1894 was overshadowed by the jibbooms of the great square-riggers tied up at their East River berths. Drays clattered along the cobbled streets, and facing the docks were rows of sailor hangouts and ship chandlers.

The East River carried all kinds of traffic in 1900. While square-riggers still picked up cargo at their piers, passengers to both Long Island Sound ports and New Jersey were serviced by steamers.

PAINTING BY CHARLES ROBERT PATTERSON

Commodore Cornelius Vanderbilt who had started as a barge deckhand, was a firm believer in the get-tough tactics. He operated with brutal skill in the port, driving all but the strongest steamer line competitors out of business. His People's Line had a fleet of nearly fifty vessels. He fought bitterly to take trade away from the Citizen's Line, owned by Daniel Drew, and the Union Line, and the North River Line. Fares from New York to Albany were drastically reduced in the 1840's as the powerful companies sought control of the trade. They went from three dollars to a dollar, then down to a dime, and from that to nothing.

The small companies disappeared, broke, unable to compete any longer. Vanderbilt's line kept in business by charging high prices for staterooms and meals. Then, gradually, passenger fares were returned. Similar tactics were employed to take over the lucrative Long Island Sound service, and the coastwise lines. Most small companies were forced to sell out to a monopoly directed by Vanderbilt.

Masters, mates and engineers, put on the beach after the mergers, looked for work in the transatlantic steamers. Sail was not for them, so there were few jobs available. No steamships were operated in the transatlantic service by an American company until the organization of the Ocean Steam Navigation Company of New York in 1847. It owned only two vessels at first, the side-wheelers *Washington* and *Herman,* built by Westervelt and Mackay in an East River yard.

Both ships were bark-rigged, with long hulls, square sterns, and built throughout of wood. They continued a strange tradition of painting a broad white stripe just below their main deck bulwarks, broken by black-painted "gun ports," although there were no guns, and the ports themselves were false. *Washington* was 230 feet long, with a 39-foot beam, a 31-foot draft. Her engine, and that of *Herman* were identical, of the side lever type.

The company operated them on a twice-a-month schedule to Bremen, with a call at Cowes in both directions. They were supported by a United States Mail contract of $200,000 a year, granted to offset the subsidies paid by foreign governments to their transatlantic service ships. *Washington* started her first voyage June 1, 1847, and *Herman* followed her March 21, 1848.

PAINTING BY CHARLES ROBERT PATTERSON

Another view of the Port of New York at the turn of the century, showing the lower bay with sailing ships at anchor, waiting to be towed to their docks. (Right) An unusual photograph showing a coastwise schooner using tide and wind to negotiate the tricky currents beneath the Williamsburg Bridge.

Washington took out with her an agent of the Post Office Department who established an international system of postage with the European governments. Letter postage from New York to Europe was 24 cents per half ounce or less; weights of a half ounce to an ounce cost 48 cents, and 15 cents more for every additional half ounce. Newspapers and pamphlets cost three cents apiece, and mail of every sort went in both directions. But Congress failed to renew the mail contracts in 1858. The two ships were taken off the run and sent into the Pacific trade.

Most of the men who served in them went with the ships to the West Coast. At-

tachment to a vessel for sentimental reasons was not confined solely to the old sailing ship men for new traditions were growing. The new type of seaman had taken over a lot of the old ways, although unshaken in his preference for steam.

The only profound change in shipboard life was the introduction of engineers. They were held responsible by the operators for a large share of the performance and safety of the vessel. Their qualifications were manifest, but for at least fifty years their presence in a ship was fiercely resented by the masters, the mates and even the unlicensed deck personnel. Many masters refused to have any but the most formal contact with their chief engineers, never entered the engine or fire rooms, seldom left the bridge during a voyage, and gave all orders to the engine department by telegraph or speaking tube from the wheel-house.

This hostile attitude on the part of the deck force created a long-lasting hatred. Men who worked below in a steamer came to be known as "the black gang," and it was meant as a term of contempt. Focsles, even messrooms, were kept separate. According to the men on deck, the engine department members never washed, and used buckets only to sit on while supposedly at work below.

Fights were common between members of the two departments either at sea or in port, and at the slightest pretext. It was sometimes necessary during a long and savage battle in port to call the police to stop the men. They fought each other with spanners, wrenches, fire hose nozzles, marline spikes, knives and bottles.

But many of the early engine-room officers were men of New England backgrounds, with the proverbial mechanical "bent" of their kind. They found in the deck officers a number who came from the same region, and, slowly, they settled their differences and developed mutual respect.

The work below in the crude, badly ventilated, poorly lit and dangerously cramped fire-rooms did not appeal to men of American birth. The jobs went to the wild and brawny Liverpool Irish, and Greeks, Italians, Spaniards, men who boasted that they could stand the intense heat, the dust, the gases, and the back-breaking labor.

There were as yet no American maritime unions to regulate working conditions. Most firemen and coal passers were illiterate, signed their "mark" on the ship's articles, lived to get drunk in the port of call, stay with a whore for an hour or so, return aboard and go back to the coal scoop.

Firemen and their lesser numbers, the coal passers, did not last long in the ships. A dozen years, at most, and they were gone. Tuberculosis finished them, or pneumonia, rheumatism, alcohol or venereal disease. Yet all of them were proud of their calling. Some of the Liverpool lot wore a single gold earring, knotted a clean sweat rag around their throats when they went below on watch, used soap and water and changed their underwear before they swaggered off the ship in port.

The men of the deck force remained American in a majority of the ships during the first decades of steam. But the old incentives of reasonably rapid advancement as an officer were lacking, and pay was poor, quarters crowded. Petty officers, bosuns, carpenters, quartermasters, content with what they had, stayed and cautiously saved their pay for retirement. The younger sailors became drifters, went into a coastwise schooner or a square-rigger, worked ashore for a while, and at last left the sea altogether.

The jobs were taken by foreigners who, paid less at home, were willing to accept the conditions. They were British, and Danes, and Swedes, and Finns, and a sprinkling from a dozen other nationalities. It became company policy in a number of steamship lines to hire officers of a single national origin. These men took out American citizenship eventually, but they went to their home countries for their wives, and when they retired, went there to stay.

A good many of the companies, though, recognized the difficulties inherent in such hiring practice. They kept men of American birth as the licensed personnel in their vessels, paid them sufficiently well, and advanced them whenever possible. The Pacific Mail Steamship Company, whose first steamer, *California,* left New York on October 6, 1848 to sail around the Horn to San Francisco, employed only native-born officers.

Experienced American officers were hard to find. The Pacific Mail Company needed two officers in 1851 and the senior master, Captain William Pearson, looked in vain. Finally he called in Richard L. Whiting and W. L. Dall. He interviewed the two officers in New York, hoping that they would prove suitable to command the steamers *California* and *Columbia* on voyages to the West Coast.

Both Whiting and Dall had been masters in sail, but Captain Pearson wanted to reassure himself about their qualifications for handling steamers. When he questioned Whiting about his steamer experience, Whiting replied, "The same that you have yourself, sir—going on the ferry to Hoboken."

Dall was asked the same question, and gave a more blunt answer.

"None at all," he said. "But I'm engaged to be married to a lady in Hoboken, and I hope to learn something in traveling back and forth on the ferry."

The two men became very successful steamship masters, and sailed the Pacific for years. They were among the group of deck officers and engineers who helped expand the company's service to Honolulu, Japan, China and Australia. But the early years were extremely hard, and demanded a great deal of skillful seamanship and outright daring.

William H. Webb had built *California* and *Panama,* the third company vessel. *Oregon,* the second, was another East River ship, from the Smith and Dimon yard. All three when leaving New York were loaded with material for buildings, shop tools, duplicate machine parts, and supplies of every description that might be needed for vessel repair on the West Coast.

The Pacific Mail Steamship line was founded by a New York contractor, George Law, famous for his enterprise. He had been quick to see the need for steam navigation in the Pacific. His first move was to create a service for the California gold-seekers who wanted to avoid the Cape Horn route. He founded in 1847 the United States Mail Steamship Company, and right afterward the Panama Railroad Company and the Pacific Mail Steamship Company.

Law and his associates received a $480,000 mail subsidy from the government, and opened their service at the stinking, malaria-foul port of Aspinwall on the Caribbean side of the Isthmus of Panama. They sent the gold-seekers, the mail and high premium cargo forty miles up the Chagres River in two very small side-wheel steam-

The *Rhode Island* of the Providence Line was originally built as a steamer. It was an unprofitable venture and the owners rebuilt her as a schooner.

ers, *Orus* and *Gorgona*. Where the steamers pulled into the bank, Cimaroon guides waited with mules. The rest of the trip across the Isthmus was through the jungle, over the trail that was to become the right-of-way of the Panama Railroad Company. Seagoing steamers waited at anchor off Panama City on the Pacific side, taking on the passengers and cargo from lighters for the run north.

A first class ticket through to San Francisco cost $600. Deck passage was half that price. There was capacity passenger business from the start, and the Pacific Mail added steadily to its fleet of ships, until there were sixteen in operation on various runs. Coal was very expensive, though, and was shipped either from the East Coast or from Europe. The company paid an average price of twenty dollars a ton, and in emergency as much as fifty dollars a ton. Steamer masters and chief engineers held many anxious conferences about engine performance, fuel consumption, and the sea miles left to the next coaling station.

Pacific Mail Company masters led a strenuous life in general. More than a few of the passengers headed for California were hard-bitten men. Gamblers and gun-fighters were among them, and often when a steamer arrived in San Francisco, her brig was full. French whores sent out by the hundreds with their *madames* and slick-haired, swaggering pimps were a constant source of trouble. The pimps, known as *maquereaux,* which the Americans shortened to "macs", were knife-fighters, and fast to take offense if one of their charges offered herself on a free lance basis. Captains were sometimes forced to go below, revolver in hand, into the passenger quarters, and restore peace, or inspect a badly cut up body, or make an arrest.

Central American politics created another series of problems. Threats were made to commandeer vessels, or they were held in port until various fines had been paid. Suggestions were made by local officials about how cargo could be smuggled and landed without manifest in the middle of the night. Then there were officials out of favor with the government, who were forced to flee before they were shot. They came aboard armed, desperate and in extreme haste.

Pursuit from shore was common in such cases, because those who fled were usually in possession of large sums of money that belonged to the government. Shots were fired, and orders shouted to stop the ship.

For many Pacific Mail masters their early years in sail seemed tranquil in comparison with this. But this was the turmoil of change. Too busy with their immediate problems, few of them realized the true meaning of their efforts. They were making the clippers obsolete, destroying the Cape Horn run, ending the domination of sail.

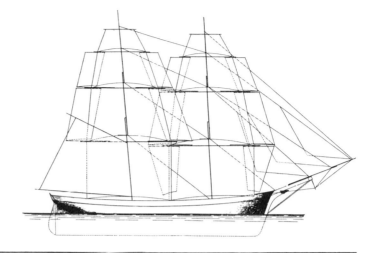

CHAPTER ELEVEN

The Gloucestermen

. . . the wind was fair over her quarter, right where she liked it.

AMONG THE FISHERMEN UP AND DOWN the American coast, and particularly in the New England region, sail power continued well into the twentieth century. The men liked the schooner, finding it both seaworthy and easy to handle in the close, dangerous waters along the coast. During the nineteenth century schooners were built by the hundreds in local yards in Maine and on down the coast to Virginia, with Baltimore architects giving clipper lines to the vessels they designed.

There have been many claims that the schooner originated in America, with the inventor usually named. He is supposed to have been a Gloucester captain who yelled, as his newly launched vessel slid gracefully from the ways, "See how she schoons!"

But it is an easily provable fact that the schooner was in use in northern European waters long before the "schooning" date; and there are records of this type of vessel being·used in early American colonial times.

Two-masted and three-masted ships were preferred, particularly by the Gloucester fishermen who made their living on the Grand and Georges Banks off Nova Scotia, and farther out on the north Atlantic. Nova Scotians and New Foundlanders, in the same trade, welcomed the rig, and built their own sturdy craft. Men who fished inshore along the rough, tide-devilled Nova Scotian coast thought so much of the schooner design they sailed two-masters of open hull construction that were only about twenty feet over-all, and quite likely the smallest in service anywhere.

The fast, slender-lined schooner *Arthur James* leaves Gloucester, Massachusetts, on her maiden voyage in 1905, bound for sea as a mackerel seiner.

Gloucester, Massachusetts, became the foremost schooner port after the War of 1812, trading in cod, haddock, halibut and mackerel. There were, by 1850, more than 400 ships sailing out of it, and 5,000 men served aboard them. Confederate raiders wrecked the fleet in the Civil War; survivors from vessels lost on the Georges Bank vehemently cursed a bark-rigged steamer that appeared suddenly out of the fog. She used her deck guns, systematically sank every vessel within range, gave no help to wounded or drowning men, then steamed away to the northward.

The Gloucester fleet was rebuilt at the end of the war, and flourished. But in the period from 1861 to 1881, when men still hand-lined for the catch from dories sent out by the schooners, there were frightful losses. The average was 89 men a year lost at sea, and most of them were young, the heads of families. Gloucester, with a population of around 25,000, very keenly missed them. Still men kept on sailing to the banks in any kind of weather.

During what was to be called "The Black Night," 275 men were lost. This was on the Grand Banks; and several times, on the Georges, more than 100 Gloucestermen were drowned. The record remained grim: 160 men on another night of storm, fog and fatal collision; 140 men on another; then, twice, more than a third of Gloucester's fleet of forty vessels went down, with all hands.

The fatalities were expected, and the reasons for them well understood. Even when the slow, clumsy hand-line fishing gave way to the trawl fashion around 1880, the lives of dorymen who worked the banks were in nearly constant peril. It took two men to handle a trawl, a long, heavy line that carried lighter, shorter lines at about three-foot intervals with the hooks at their ends. The heavy line lay on the bottom, a small anchor to hold it. When it was taken in, one of the dorymen stood in the bow and hauled, and gaffed the hooked halibut, which weighed between 100–200 pounds. His partner crouched in the waist of the dory and coiled the line; he was also responsible for the boat if she started to broach to a sea and capsize.

Fog often trapped the dorymen miles away from their ships. There were always strong tides to confuse them, and when they were headed by adverse winds, they were forced to row great distances, as much as 100 and 150 miles. They suffered from exposure, and lack of food, and in the wintertime the boats were often encumbered by thick sheaths of ice.

The early Gloucester schooners were round-bowed, with square sterns and full waists, built for seaworthiness and carrying capacity. Then, as the fresh fish market developed and the cargoes were no longer salted down at sea, there was need for speed and sharper lines. The first vessel in port got the top price.

"Make 'em sharp!" the fishermen told the builders.

Another of the Gloucester fishing schooners, the *Harry Belden*, heads for sea. On the fore trestle-trees, a sailor stands ready to loosen the topsail.

A few of the new designs became so extreme the vessels drove straight under the oncoming waves, and sometimes never regained the surface.

Modifications were made in the designs, and Gloucester ships were once more famous for their seaworthiness. Captain Maurice Whalen in his straight-stemmed schooner *Harry Belden,* which measured 100 feet over-all, established a memorable run from westward of Georges Bank. He sailed her from the North Shoal to Boston Lightship in ten hours, a distance of 154 sea miles. But the record was improved upon by Captain Tommy Bohlen.

Bohlen, another Gloucesterman, sailed *Nannie Bohlen* from Cape Sable to Gloucester, a distance of 222 sea miles, in 14 hours and 25 minutes. His schooner was 117 feet over-all, and her speed for the run, 15.6 knots, was never equalled by any vessel of her tonnage. Bohlen said about her, "The wind was fair over her quarter, where she liked it."

Common practice when coming home with a load of fish from The Banks was to sail the schooners with the lee rail under, the deck-house just about awash.

"Keep her full!" the helmsmen were told.

That meant no luffing, no hauling off from the wind when a squall hit, and in heavy winter weather, the helmsman had to be lashed to the wheel. Schooner pelted past schooner into Gloucester harbor, carrying topsails and jibs, foresails and main-sails until well inside Eastern Point and only dropping them at the last moment to go to anchor.

The Chesapeake bugeye, *Lizzie J. Cox,* at anchor in a dead calm. Some of the grace of the famous Baltimore clippers can be seen in her lines. The bow-on view shows details of her handsome fore structure.

A winter scene at Boston's T Wharf, with the fishing fleet in from the Grand Banks.

But despite the skill of the crews, despite the fine qualities of the vessels, the terrible danger still persisted out on The Banks; Georges Bank was the worst one. What the men feared there was the combination of a Northeast gale and a snow storm. Shoal water reached North, South and West, and the only way out for a vessel in rough weather was to the eastward. Snow could limit visibility to half a ship's length in daylight, and at night obscure everything, hiding from sight vessels that lay right alongside.

Riding lights were unseen. Foghorns were blunted to a feeble squawk. Men going along the deck bumped into masts and each other, tripped, fell, and barely heard their curses. When the powerful tide changed and the wind velocity increased, a second anchor would do little good. There were usually about forty ships in the fishing fleet, all of them near enough to cause collision.

Collision, in a Northeaster that blew more than fifty miles an hour, usually ended in the loss of the ships involved, and their crews. Rescue by other vessels was all but impossible. So men stood watch beside the anchor hawser, ready to pay out slack on the windlass when a ship loomed in the wavering white snow, or even the corner of a topsail showed. They strained to hear sounds, trying to calculate movement, to figure out where their neighbors might be, and what their own drift had become. One man held an axe, poised to cut the hawser at the last second before disaster. He was rarely given sufficient warning, and could only strike a single blow.

The schooner *Leona M. Thurlow* coming home to Gloucester, Massachusetts.

Back in Gloucester, most of the widows and children never knew just how their men died. They understood a capsized dory, and collision in fog, and the ice floes that the halibut fleet met in the spring. The rest, often conjecture, was given them by survivors, men who had miraculously escaped a similar death.

During the last years of the nineteenth century, a moving custom gradually arose among the Gloucester widows. Once a year, in August, they gathered to hold a ceremony for the men who had been lost.

At first the ceremony was held in one of the churches. But the crowds soon became too big for the little church. The people then gathered at the westerly end of Main Street, in the park there that is dominated by the tall bronze statue of the fisherman in his oilskins, sea-boots and sou'wester hat.

A wreath is placed at the monument, and then people go to the bridge over The Cut, the narrow canal that allows the Squam River to flow into the harbor. The names of the missing men are read. Formal wreaths and bunches of field flowers are lowered into the water. Captains' widows in summer dresses stand beside Portuguese women dressed in full, black mourning. The prayers are recited one year by a Protestant minister, the next by a Catholic priest. While the flowers move on the ebb tide to sea, the Twenty-third Psalm is sung, and that is the end.

Losses in the Gloucester fleet are far less today than they were sixty or seventy years ago, although they still occur. The reduction in the toll came around 1900 with the introduction of auxiliary power to the sailing ships. At first the motors were put in to help the sails. In the end they replaced them. Captain Saul Jacobs who had spent many perilous years on The Banks under sail, built the auxiliary schooner *Helen Gould Miller,* and took her mackerel seining.

There were almost no wind-driven vessels sailing without auxiliaries from Gloucester by 1920, and by 1940 there were just a few salt-bankers, working 800, 1,000 and 1,200 miles from home. But they did not last long, and with them went the sail tradition that had begun with the first colonists in the Massachusetts Bay region. Several carefully arranged races between the beautiful Lunenburg, Nova Scotia schooner *Bluenose* and the equally handsome Gloucester schooner *Columbia* failed to revive interest.

The last wind-propelled vessel to serve on the Grand Banks without auxiliary power was the Portuguese three-masted gaff-head schooner *Ana Maria.* She had been built in Dundee back in 1873, and rebuilt for cod fishing in 1924, but power was not installed. She was lost in 1958.

Now, in Gloucester, it is hard to find husky young men willing to serve in a diesel-powered trawler. Gloucester has become mainly a port of memory.

MODEL BY C. DAVIES

The model of the *Columbia* shows the graceful hull design that made the Gloucester schooners prize sailers. Yet with all their speed and ease of handling, they could not compete with steam or diesel powered ships.

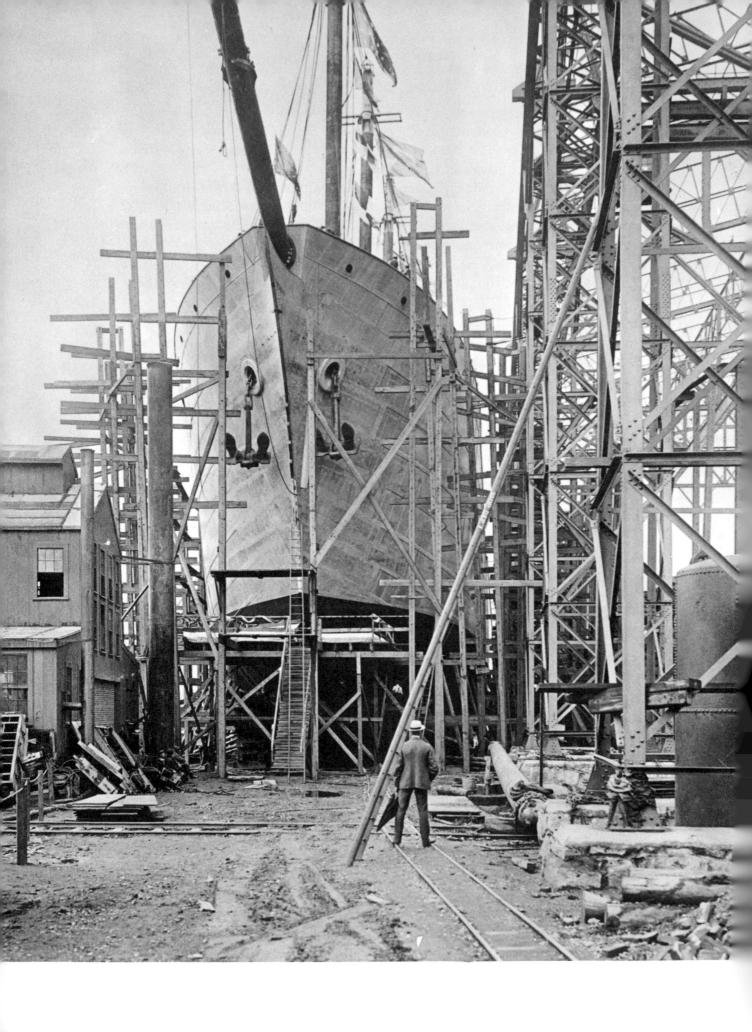

The story of the *Thomas W. Lawson,* the only seven-masted schooner ever built, began in the shipyards at Fore River, Massachusetts. It was launched July 10, 1902, and while a gala crowd watched the christening, workmen stood by to knock the wedges out and send the ship sliding into the water.

Her sails spread to the wind, the *Thomas W. Lawson* was a majestic sight at sea. Nevertheless, she was clumsy and difficult to handle, a doomed ship from the first.

Designed to be the greatest cargo-carrying sailing ship, she seldom found enough cargo to make her voyages profitable. Eventually she was converted into an oil tanker.

The end came in 1908. The *Thomas W. Lawson* breaking up below Bishop's Rock Lighthouse, off the Scilly Islands. Her crew of fifteen went down with the ship.

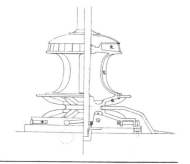

CHAPTER TWELVE

Great Lakes and Deepwater Schooners

. . . her crew were gulls, noisy in the remnants of her rigging.

For a century sail power dominated the trade on the Great Lakes. The first of the Lake schooners, *Nancy,* was built in 1789 at Detroit, Michigan. Others followed and within a few years a brisk trade had grown up to and from the lakeside cities. Then, in 1818, the first Lakes steamer, *Walk-in-the-Water,* sailed from Black Rock, just outside Buffalo, New York. The steamer proved to be far more efficient on the rivers between the lakes, and predictions were made that the schooners would soon be forced out of business.

That prediction came true, but it was half-a-century in coming. For the local shipyards began to build schooners with square-rigged topsails on the foremasts, and steam tugs were used in the rivers when the wind and current were not right. Most of the schooners were two-masted, and rarely over 100 feet in length. Their main cargoes were wheat from Lake Superior, carried to Buffalo and then transferred to barges for the Erie Canal, and timber for construction to almost every city in the Midwest. The schooners proved to be fairly cheap cargo carriers.

Chicago was built with schooner-hauled timber. The greatest sawdust pile in the world was believed to have been at Muskegon, Michigan. The schooners loaded there for the run across Lake Michigan, took deck loads of fresh pine until there was hardly clearance for the fore and main booms.

"Timber out and hosses back!" was a well-known toast in Muskegon saloons in the big years right after the Civil War. The "hosses" they were toasting walked on two legs.

The brigantine *Columbia* carried the first cargo of iron ore from Lake Superior through the Soo Locks on August 17, 1855.

The schooners delivered the timber and returned from Chicago with reinforcements for the logging teams. The men were usually drunk. Old-timers claimed that on a dark night they could smell a Muskegon-bound schooner long before they could see her.

The competition was stiff between the various schooner companies, but only the Blue Bottom line became so well-known that a chantey was sung about it. The chorus went:

> *Watch 'em, catch 'em!*
> *Jump up in the Jupu Ju!*
> *Give her the sheets and let her rip,*
> *We're the boys to crowd her through.*
> *Oh, you should ha' heard 'em holler*
> *As the wind went howling free,*
> *For we beat the fleet from Buffalo—*
> *Buffalo to Milwaukee.*

But steam power came to the Great Lakes, too; and sailing ships had to give way to the new. Captain Alex McDougall launched the first of his whaleback steamers in 1881. Her designation was simply #101, and she was towed from Two Harbors to Cleveland with a load of iron ore. The schooners could not match her bulk carrying capacity. They lost trade steadily, no matter how hard they were driven, and after 1900 there were very few of them left.

Lucia A. Simpson, the last schooner in service on Lake Michigan. She was built in 1875 at Manitowoc, Wisconsin, and spent most of her long career hauling lumber.

One of the last of the Lake Schooners, sodden, sadly listing, but with her topsail yard still crossed, lay for years on a mudbank in Lake St. Clair above Detroit. Her crew were gulls, noisy in the remnants of her rigging.

Shipyards in Maine continued building big, deepwater schooners long after the steamer competition had become too keen on the Great Lakes. As early as 1880, the *William L. White,* a four-master, had proven successful in coastal trade. She was easier to handle when sailing close-hauled than a square-rigged ship of the same tonnage, and she needed fewer men in her crew. Then the first five-master, *Governor Ames,* was built in 1888, and in 1900 the first six-master, *George W. Wells,* came off the ways. They were followed, in 1902, by the only schooner with more than six masts ever to be built. She was the cumbersome and slab-sided *Thomas W. Lawson,* built with seven masts and the expectation on the part of her owners that she would be a successful bulk cargo carrier.

But ships of her massive fore and aft rig were found to be very slow and clumsy when it was necessary to claw off shore in a storm. The flaw in the construction often proved fatal. *Thomas W. Lawson* went on the rocks off the Scilly Islands while on a foreign voyage and was lost, with all hands.

Most of the ships of her type were wrecked or foundered in shoal waters over the years. European ship operators never accepted the type, considering them too clumsy. The owners of the American ships, except during the 1917–18 war years, kept their vessels in the coastwise trade.

One of the most dramatic of the coastwise schooner histories is that of the *Mertie B. Crowley*. She was representative of her class, and the circumstances of her loss were similar to scores of other big, bulk-carrying schooners. During an unusually heavy fog late in January, 1910, the six-master lay hove to, wallowing in heavy ocean swells and frigid, calm air off Long Island, New York. She was under the command of Captain William Haskell, with a crew of thirteen men. Mrs. Haskell was aboard as a passenger.

The schooner was North-bound for Boston, Massachusetts with a full cargo of coal. The heavy sea and the accompanying fog followed a storm during which Captain Haskell had lost his bearings. He had been on deck for thirty hours without sleep. When the weather cleared, the ship stood in close to shore under a fresh Northwest breeze.

But he and his two mates failed to establish correctly the characteristics of the

Oliver Mitchell is typical of the fine Great Lakes topsail schooners. She was built at Algonac, Michigan, in 1874.

coastal light they sighted in the darkness. They identified it as Shinnecock Light. In reality the strong Easterly set of the current had put them more than forty miles beyond it, and what they saw was a light on Block Island. The captain increased his error by setting an East-Northeast course; he expected to raise Block Island before daylight, then head around through Vineyard Sound into port.

Since he was already abreast of Block Island his course took the ship south of No Man's Land, and south of Martha's Vineyard. *Mertie B. Crowley* piled up on Great Wasque Shoal, in the mass of rips that runs for miles out to sea from the southeast corner of the Vineyard. The same heavy swell was still running, and the schooner hit hard, immediately lost her life-boats and everything loose on deck. Here, in shoal water, the action of the sea was rough, and high. Captain Haskell, his mates and sailors knew that they were in extreme danger. They had to abandon ship at once, or drown in what was left of the wreckage.

Captain Haskell went below. His wife, a small woman, was still asleep, and in her nightgown. He wrapped her in his watchcoat and rapidly climbed the companionway ladder with her in his arms. The hatches were being broken by the weight of the seas that crashed aboard. Water poured into the holds, broke bulkheads and rushed through the focsle and the main cabin.

The captain carried his wife into the fore rigging. He lashed her to the cross-trees, and then secured himself. The crew were aloft also, secured in the fore and main ratlines. But it was freezing weather; the spindrift as it struck them turned into pellets of ice. Below, on deck, the great, black, white-crested seas pounded the schooner apart. They made flinders of the deck houses, and then the ship broke in half.

The stern settled fast, the three after masts, their rigging slacked, buckled. But the three forward masts held in the perpendicular. With dawn, the people who clung to them could see the south shore of the Vineyard, three miles away. Edgartown lay snug behind the arm of Cape Pogue, the chimney smoke of the early risers pale above it. When a pilot of one of the island steamers looked out over his vessel's bridge wing, across the low hills of the island, he sighted the wreck.

This was about an hour after dawn, and word was rapidly passed ashore. The local folks immediately sought out Captain Levi Jackson. He had been famous for some years because of his disregard of personal safety. The Vineyard had given him the nickname of Ready-to-Die, which the inhabitants chose to pronounce as Ri-De-Di-Die.

Captain Jackson was without question the man to save the people aboard *Mertie B. Crowley*. He was the master of the strongly built auxiliary fishing sloop *Priscilla*, and with her had made a number of rescues. But he was still in bed when neighbors knocked on the door and told him of the schooner out on Great Wasque Shoal. The captain dressed hurriedly, ate his breakfast, and put on his double gear, seaboots and sou'wester. Then he kissed his wife and his newly born son, went down to the fish pier with the neighbors.

One of the earliest steam-driven vessels in service on the Great Lakes, the *V. H. Ketchum* was built as a schooner, then converted into a steamer. It was lost in 1906.

His crew had already heard about the schooner. They were aboard *Priscilla*, and had her prepared for sea. The powerful motor was started; jib and main were hoisted. *Priscilla* cleared the pier and started to beat around Cape Pogue to windward.

It took Captain Jackson more than an hour to round the cape under the extremely severe conditions he encountered. Then he steered through Muskeget Channel, which separates Martha's Vineyard from the smaller islands of Muskeget, Tuckernuck and Nantucket, toward the open sea. When *Priscilla* reached the southerly end of Muskeget Channel, spindrift was leaping thirty and forty feet in the air with the impact of the wind. Waves crashed ominously below, shoulder upon steep, sharp shoulder.

The channel was very narrow here between the sand bar known as Skiff's Island on the west and Muskeget on the east. During heavy weather, the seas broke clear across it, and under such conditions homeward-bound fishing schooners completely avoided it. The schooner men sailed far to the westward, around No Man's Land, and then, finally, back into Vineyard Sound.

Jackson took his chances with the channel, put the sloop through it. His men bailed so fast they could not take time to look up and watch him steer. Spindrift hurled over the boat in great, rough gusts of pellets as big as hail stones. Ice formed on deck, and on the men's oilskins and their sou'wester brims even as they worked. Bent, crouched on their knees, bailing scoops and buckets in their hands, they listened in the storm sounds for the steady thud-thud-thud of *Priscilla's* motor. If that ever faltered, no matter what Jackson did at the helm, they would almost instantly drown.

Wasque Point, at the southeast corner of the Vineyard, stretched in a huge semi-circular shoal formation for five miles out to seaward, the outer rim an awful

maelstrom of breakers. It would be impossible for any vessel the size of *Priscilla* to live there. But the foundering schooner was at the westerly end of the shoal, where it curved back inshore towards the Vineyard.

Jackson knew that he could not cut across the shoal to the wreck. A much bigger vessel than his, the fishing schooner *Viking,* had tried it some hours before, and very nearly went under. That was Jackson's fear now as he battled the sloop through the cross seas, the eddies and sudden, mysterious currents of the channel. The sloop was flung so far out of the water by the action of the seas that when she came down again, she might well keep right on, bury her bow, and pitchpole herself, mast following bow, and stern following mast.

Jackson eased *Priscilla* very gradually from the channel. He beat to seaward using the very small lee of Skiff's Island, holding his course between it and Wasque Point. When he had sea room, he hauled around so that he headed westward, parallel to the edge of the shoal. *Mertie B. Crowley* lay on the westerly bank of the shoal, about a mile inside the buoy that marked the southern end. Jackson took a careful bearing on her when he was abreast, then stared out to sea.

The United States Revenue cutter *Acushnet* was offshore. She was of too deep draft to enter the shoal waters. Her lifeboat might have reached the wreck, but would never return from it. The rescue job was for men like Jackson. They knew all of these rips and slues and shoals by heart. Levi Jackson had learned them from his father, and his father from Levi's grandfather.

Jackson began to bring the sloop around, head her into the quarter mile of furious surf that separated him from the schooner. *Priscilla* was close enough now

132

The three-masted schooner in the foreground is the *Nova Queen*, built at Advocate, Nova Scotia, in 1919, and missing since December, 1934. In the background are two unidentified vessels apparently identical to *Nova Queen*.

The Maine-built, four-masted schooner *E. Starr Jones* in a fresh breeze. Built at Thomaston in 1904, wrecked on July 25, 1919 off Rio Grande do Sul.

Alice M. Lawrence hard aground on Tuckernuck Shoal off Nantucket Island, 1914. She went down on top of the wreck of the French schooner *Van Guilder,* sunk thirty years earlier on the same spot. In 1926 the British schooner *Unique* wrecked herself on the submerged hull of the *Alice M. Lawrence.*

Two views of the deck of the *Alice M. Lawrence* as the wreckers stripped her of everything of value. Looking toward the bow (left) and toward the stern (right).

so that he could make out the figures in the rigging, distinguish the huddled, ice-sheathed body of the captain's wife.

Priscilla gathered speed, thrust on by the awful force of the breakers. The sloop buried herself in half her length, brought water back solid to the cockpit coaming, then shook herself, staggered clear and rose and once more drove forward. Now she was past the sunken stern of the schooner and abreast of the fore part. Jackson put the wheel over and tried to move upwind towards the hulk. But he could not bring the sloop in alongside; that would be suicidal. A single breaker recoil would smash her against the schooner, and she would go with all hands.

Jackson, stooped over the wheel box, ice white on his mittens where they gripped the spokes, looked forward into the faces of his crew. He did not say anything; the men could not hear him anyway. But they nodded. Four of them put their dories in the water. They were Patrick Kelly, Eugene Benefit, Louis Doncett, and Henry Kelly. Rowing separate courses, they started for the schooner to take off her people.

Mrs. Haskell, the captain's wife, was the first to make the attempt. She jumped with a line around her, in the exact split second that one of the dories rose with the wave and was almost parallel with the schooner's main deck. They let go the line on deck, and she landed squarely on the narrow bottom of the dory. She fainted, lying there in the slosh of water, and afterwards Levi Jackson said that was a good thing.

"She was a little woman, but with her clothes soaked, she weighed a ton, and we had to grab her by the arms, the hair, the legs, everywhere we could get a hold, and then we had all we could do to hoist her aboard the *Priscilla*."

All the rest of the people were taken straight from the schooner to the sloop except the steward. He missed his jump from the rail, and reaching out, Patrick Kelly grasped him, tried to pull the man into the dory. But the steward, in panic, capsized the dory. The craft was hurled at once against the schooner and crushed. Kelly rode the crest of a wave and tumbled from it into the schooner's rigging and desperately hung onto it. Then the steward, also flung upward on a comber, appeared at the bow. His shipmates reached out and grabbed him, and he, too, was safe.

It was a long and dangerous job for the three remaining dories to haul the rest of the schooner people and Kelly to the sloop. But the transfer was made with Captain Haskell in the last boat to make the trip. Then *Priscilla* began the exceedingly hazardous homeward run.

Jackson was given no choice. It was impossible for him to head to seaward against the breakers. He had to go with them, hold them astern, and run the full seven miles across the shoal to Muskeget Channel. Some of the shoal water was only three feet deep, but Jackson followed the gullies, and *Priscilla* survived. He navigated her into the channel and on to Edgartown.

Many of the schooners met a fate similar to that of *Mertie B. Crowley;* not all of them were as lucky. And faith in the power of wind and sail was fast vanishing from the sea.

Waiting at the piers in Oakland, California, until there is enough cargo for a profitable voyage. Steel hulls were safer than wooden ones, but wind-driven ships still could not compete with the reliable schedules of steamers.

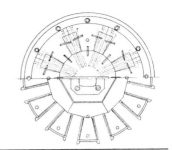

CHAPTER THIRTEEN

The Shame of Rum Row

. . . it was a strange and drab end for the proud American schooner.

Shipping needs during World War I brought back into commission practically all of the old-time sailing vessels. Among them were more than a hundred American schooners. These were sent mainly to the French port of Brest, carrying bulk cargo for the American Expeditionary Force.

The people of Brest had never before seen a fleet like it. They came down to the quayside to stare at the big schooners, a number of them four-masters. Their own craft, which sailed to the Grand Banks, were half the size of these. And the schooner crews were also an extraordinary collection, worth just as much interest as the ships.

Many of the men were Negroes recruited in the West Indies. Their shipmates were Americans, Swedes, Norwegians, Finns, Danes, Spaniards, Greeks and Italians. They lived in the sailing ship tradition. Chanties were sung in the dockside *cafés;* marble table tops were slapped as though they were drum heads. Then men danced with any of the women who were willing, and any of the men, and finally by themselves. It was as though the ghosts of all the men who ever sailed the seas had come back for one last fling.

Some of the big American schooners were kept in service on the East Coast after the war. They ran out of Hampton Roads, Virginia, through the 1920's with cargoes of coal, and hauled lumber and any other bulk cargo their owners could find. On the West Coast, they went back to the timber trade, or hauled sugar from the Hawaiian Islands. The ships were a familiar sight at City Island, above New York City, waiting for the right tide to run the East River; and on the West Coast they could be seen along the docks at Bremerton, Everett, Spokane, Bellingham, and Port Townsend. The West Coast crews said, "Any place they got a sawmill and a dock, we tie up and load."

The powerful, sea-worn French bark *Rochambeau* docking at San Francisco after her maiden voyage. The clock tower in the background is on the Ferry Building at

But the schooners were finished in the early 1930's as working vessels. The last served out their time on Rum Row during Prohibition, just outside the twelve mile limit, helping to smuggle whiskey into the United States.

The finest of the ships in the Rum Row fleet was *Arethusa*. She belonged to Captain William McCoy, known among the bootleggers as "the real McCoy" because of his honest dealing, and by all accounts a very good sailor. McCoy was a graduate of the Pennsylvania Maritime Academy, and had served aboard the academy's square-rigger *Saratoga*.

When Prohibition came into effect, McCoy was in Florida trying to save his family's motor boat service between Palm Beach and Fort Myers that was being threatened by the new bus lines. McCoy convinced his brother to sell out, took the money from the sale and went north to find a schooner with which he could go into rum-running. He found her in Gloucester.

She was the 90-foot *Henry L. Marshall,* of white pine construction, designed and built for the fishing trade in the James yard at Essex, Massachusetts. She carried

138

the foot of Market Street. Built at Nantes, France, in 1902, the *Rochambeau* was wrecked in 1911 off Noumea, New Caledonia.

a pair of pole masts and had a semi-knockabout rig; twin propellers and a motor gave her a speed of up to seven knots. McCoy bought her for $16,000, spent another $4,000 to refit her. While the work was being done, he stayed in Gloucester.

Old-timers around the port told him of another schooner named *Arethusa*. They showed him an oil painting of her, hung above the street door of the Gloucester Master Mariners Association quarters. McCoy was interested. *Arethusa* was off on the Grand Banks, commanded by Captain Clayton Morissey, a famous sail-crowder. When *Arethusa* came back with a haul, McCoy was waiting at the Gorton Pew wharf.

He watched her come into the harbor and slip alongside the dock. The handsome, black-hulled vessel, lean and sturdy, caught his fancy. McCoy promised himself that he would buy the two-master. But his money was already spent on the *Marshall*, and the East Coast Fisheries Company which owned *Arethusa* wanted a good price for her.

McCoy sailed *Henry L. Marshall* to Nassau and put her in the rum-running trade

A muster of square-riggers lost during World War I. The three vessels in the foreground were the Russian-owned iron bark *Finland,* formerly the *King Arthur,* built in 1887 at Dundee; steel bark *Estes,* Norwegian owned, built at Glasgow, Scotland, in 1891; and the iron bark *Morna* built at Birkenhead in 1877. The *Finland* was wrecked at the mouth of the Loire River, France, in 1918. Both the *Este* and the *Morna* were sunk by enemy action in 1917.

with a crew of tough Gloucester fishermen, and did well. After a few trips he had enough money to buy *Arethusa,* and went north to make the purchase. But in Gloucester he learned the company which owned her was out of business; *Arethusa* was laid up in Rockland, Maine.

McCoy kept on going, reached Rockland and found the vessel. He boarded her and found *Arethusa* more to his liking than ever. McCoy had his faults, but he knew a good ship when he saw it. He talked to the owners and settled on a price of $21,000. Then he sailed her to East Gloucester and spent another $11,000 for a refit. *Arethusa* got all new rigging and sails, and topmasts were sent up, and a raking bowsprit shipped.

The bowsprit would let her set a flying jib, and he gave her a new motor, painted her hull white instead of black. All this added to the bill, so McCoy studied her below with great care. He changed her bulkhead plan which made it possible to carry more liquor as cargo. Then he hired a veteran New England schooner master, Captain Albert Gott, and a crew of Gloucestermen who devoutly disliked Prohibition. With a full suit of new canvas bent on, *Arethusa* stood out from Gloucester to Nassau, McCoy at the wheel.

Perhaps McCoy was aware of the cruel irony of it all. Certainly he knew *Arethusa* was as fine and beautiful a schooner as had ever sailed. And he had no illusions about the rum-running business. The best of the schooners was embarking on the worst of the sea trade.

He tried her on the wind, and off, running on a broad reach or pointed close to the wind, with her big jumbo jib set and without it. She sailed fine. McCoy regretted only one thing about her. He found, after reading the British ship registry list in Nassau, that there was already an *Arethusa* on it. For protective reasons, if caught with contraband in American territorial waters, she would need British register. He renamed her *Tomoka*. But she was always called her original name by McCoy, and by anybody who got to know her well on Rum Row.

McCoy had a capacity of 5,000 cases of liquor aboard *Arethusa*. But he had enough cash to buy only 1,000. He went to George Murphy, a broad-beamed American friend who had become one of the most successful of the Nassau liquor dealers. Murphy extended credit. The liquor was bottled, labelled and sent to the packing tables. Six bottles, each in its paper wrapping, were stacked in a compact pyramidal form, straw placed around them and a close cover of burlap stitched with double sail twine. Negro women sang hymns in sweet voices while they packed the liquor.

Arethusa was loaded and put out to sea. The weather was fair as she ran northward. Eight days after he cleared Nassau, McCoy picked up the powerful beam of Fire Island Lightship and worked his way to an anchorage in the middle of the Rum Row congregation. The fleet now maintained position a full twenty miles offshore, after a number of Coast Guard arrests and seizures within the three mile limit. Here the big white cutters did not pay much attention to the vessels on the Row; their real purpose was to catch the small craft that came out from shore to buy the liquor and smuggle it into the country.

McCoy did not have a consignee for his cargo. He sold over the side of the schooner to any buyer who pitched his money to the deck. And there were plenty of buyers. They tossed packets of neatly rolled bills clasped within a rubber band. Then the liquor was handed over and they disappeared into the night. The cargo sold fast. McCoy was back in Nassau eighteen days after he had left, and his financial condition was much better.

The trade continued to grow and McCoy's prosperity went along with it. On every voyage he did a bit better than on the previous one. But then, in the winter of 1922, McCoy began to see trouble ahead. Real tough types began to appear in Nassau. They were hoodlums and hijackers, and made little effort to hide the fact. There were some mean dockside fights on Bay Street at night. McCoy, a big and very strong man, was forced to take care of himself, or get killed.

Now when he sailed north with a cargo of 5,700 cases of liquor—much more than he usually carried—he kept a careful watch for the seagoing hijackers he might meet on Rum Row. *Arethusa* had a fine run with the excessive load. The crew was made up of big-fisted Finns. McCoy had practically shanghaied them from a lumber schooner. But the men appreciated the customs that had been established aboard the rum-runners and, once at sea, they asked for the liquor rack.

The handsome fishing schooner *Rob Roy* was built at Essex, Massachusetts, in 1900 and fast became famous for her speed and beauty. Her lines were soon repeated in many other vessels. The German U-156 torpedoed and sank the *Rob Roy* off Seal Island, Nova Scotia, on August 3, 1918.

McCoy went below and brought up the rack which he set in front of the helmsman. It contained four bottles from which the men could choose: wine, rum, rye and Scotch. He had seen a fair amount of schooners in his time, McCoy thought, and still, not until Prohibition had this custom existed. The man at the wheel could get woggle-eyed drunk, drain all four bottles if he wished. And there was always a man in every crew these days who would try to drink everything in sight.

While *Arethusa* ran on to the northward, logging a good twelve knots by her taffrail log, McCoy remained uneasy. He had violated American law in various ways during his rum-running voyages. There was also the problem of the hoodlums who had begun to infest the trade. They were called the "go-through guys" because they were willing to shoot their way through anything. McCoy had furnished *Arethusa* with a tripodmount machine-gun and some high power rifles against their possible arrival on Rum Row. But with the crew he carried he doubted if much resistance would be offered. The sailors would go where the most money, or the most liquor, was promised.

Typical of the last days of sailing ships, the *M. Vivian Peirce* (top, left) was converted to a bulkhead in 1940 at Astoria, Long Island, New York. The *E.S. Newman* (top, right) hauled coal, competing with the railroads for bulk cargo. The Alaska Packer Fleet (bottom) was laid up at Alameda, California.

A dockside view of *Katie D. Seavey* showing the deck cargo reaching almost to the sidelights in the rigging. Just enough space has been left at the bow to work her windlass and handle the anchors.

A heavy southwesterly storm caught *Arethusa* when she was 300 miles from Cape Hatteras, and during it McCoy was forced to exert all of his seamanly skill. His sailing master, an old Royal Navy veteran named Crosby, was struck from aloft by a block while he relieved McCoy at the wheel. Crosby died of his injury while the schooner was still in the storm, and McCoy was so disturbed that he turned over the burial service to the cook. After *Arethusa* reached Rum Row and anchored, McCoy realized that he was nearly finished with the trade.

The bootleggers on the beach and the "go-through guys" made the real profit. His cargo was worth $171,000, and was one of the most valuable to be delivered on the Row. Ashore it would be sold for double that, and then the price would be doubled again by the bootleggers. The final price would be $684,000, a fortune for any man, but one that would never belong to him.

McCoy left the trade still hunted by the law, and lost in Florida real estate the money he had made running rum. Both *Arethusa* and *Henry L. Marshall* were sold, and disappeared from the Row. Some few dilapidated old fore-and-afters were kept going until Prohibition was repealed. But they were a menace to coastal navigation more than anything else, and a number of them were cut down by liners approaching New York at night. Their crews, drunk or asleep, died with little knowledge of what had happened.

It was a strange and drab end for the proud American schooner.

The *Lizzie Brewster* moving slowly in fair weather. The lumber on the deck was stowed in the customary, economical manner that badly cramped the crew.

Two photographs of the *Olivebank*, one of the most famous of the last square-riggers. Built in Glasgow, Scotland, in 1892, *Olivebank* had the traditional false gunports painted on her sides while sailing under the British flag. In 1924, no longer economically profitable and in bad condition, the vessel was sold to the Erikson Line of Finland. The end came for the *Olivebank* during World War II when she struck a mine.

146

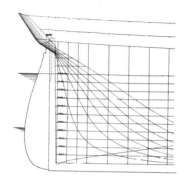

CHAPTER FOURTEEN

The Last Commercial Sail Ships

*. . . in the early 1930's more than twenty square-rigged ships
carried wheat from Australia to England.*

A SENSE OF ROMANTIC longing brought the young men to the sea, and the itch
for adventure, and in some cases poverty, and the pressing need for work. Right to the
end of the sailing ship era, as late as 1934, there were plenty of husky teen-age
European boys, and even a number of girls of the same age, willing to go to sea
in the Cape Horn square-riggers. So it was that the ships—not the seamen—wore
out first, and could not be replaced.

There were few jobs on sailing ships after World War II, even if such ships
could be operated with some profit. Young Åland islanders who came from Finland
and the Baltic region to form the greater part of the pre-war square-rigged crews,
began to realize at last that steam was better than sail. Their wives and sweethearts
vigorously supported the idea. The men who went to sea from the ports along the
Baltic came home a lot more often.

The decline of the square-riggers had been severe in the decades before World
War II. They were given fewer cargoes each year, and that came from the outports,
usually without regular steamer service. The rates were at least three dollars a ton
under that paid for steamship haulage. The sailing ships were poorly kept, with an
absolute minimum of new gear and canvas supplied them. For the men, life aboard,
particularly in the Cape Horn waters, was perilous; for the ships it was a drab,
drudging, monotonous existence.

A dramatic demonstration of the inevitable demise of wind-driven ships is provided by this unusual sequence of photographs snapped in mid-ocean. The bark *Viking* of the Erikson Line is being overtaken by an unidentified steamship.

Typical was *William Mitchell* of the Stewart Line, a ship built in the 1890's and sailed hard since. It was the last square-rigger under the British merchant navy red ensign to be commanded by a British master. Cargoes were hard to come by after World War I, and the best she could get was a load of spruce from Canada to Australia. From Australia she carried wheat to Callao. Discharging that, she sailed to the stinking, miserable islands off the Peruvian coast to load guano for Wilmington, North Carolina. The next charter was wheat again. It took five months to sail from Wilmington, around Cape Horn, to Port Lincoln, Australia. And so she struggled for her existence. She loaded the wheat and waddled across the Pacific, delivered the cargo to Callao, sailed up the coast of South America to Tocopilla for nitrate. When she brought this cargo to Ostend, the owners finally decided to get rid of the ship.

It was 1928, and the best offer for *William Mitchell* was $10,500—from the ship-breakers. So ended the career of a once-proud square-rigger. The last men in her crew said the ship-breakers should have had her long before.

A Glasgow ship, *Lady Ruthven,* established the record for the slowest passage around the Horn. She was 196 days from the Clyde, in Scotland, to Callao. For 92 endless days she struggled off the Horn, between 50 degrees South latitude in the Atlantic and 50 degrees South latitude in the Pacific. Her crew faced almost incredible dangers.

Lady Ruthven had her wheel smashed, and for hours in full storm she could not be steered. She lost her fore upper topsail yard, all her storm topsails were blown out, whipped into ribbons. Her boats were wrenched from their chocks and hurled

Even under a large press of sail, the *Viking* cannot keep up with the steamship. The steamer passes her easily, and within minutes, the great sailing ship is left far behind. The steamship would be on her return voyage by the time *Viking* reached port.

over the side, with them went the capstans bars, and most of her running gear. She took so much water aboard that she lay semi-submerged.

A series of storms beat her. She was thrust on to the southward, lying with a beam end under, more like a reef than a ship, and moving only with the utmost slowness, waves breaking solidly over her. But she reached 64 degrees South latitude, wallowing day after day in the iceberg track. Her food was nearly gone, and most of the fresh water spoiled; sea water had entered the tanks.

The crew cleared her, though, and bent on canvas and righted her. She sailed North, and West, into the Pacific while the pumps clanked constantly and the last of the food and fresh water were exhausted. When she came into Callao, the crew left her for good and the captain was not surprised. The ship did not deserve her name. She was certainly no lady.

Still, it was possible to recruit crews in Europe. Young Englishmen who wished to qualify as pilots in their country's service were forced to sail foreign to get their necessary square-rigger experience. Finns, Danes, Swedes, Germans, an occasional Frenchman or American, and, on the homeward-bound leg of the voyage, Australians filled out the muster. They understood the danger ahead of them for the most part, and they were willing to accept it as a challenge to their manhood.

Boys became men in the awful Cape Horn ordeal while the wind ships, usually in ballast, bucked against the prevailing westerly gales. The price paid by the crews was extreme. *Archibald Russell* lost two boys in 1928, swept from her jibboom. *Killoran* gave two, knocked overside from the unprotected wheel in a 1930 gale. *Lowhill, Penang* and *Lingard* each lost one from aloft. Two from *Ponape* were washed overside, and beriberi aboard *Olivebank,* caused by poor food, took the lives of four.

There was very little romance in this. Able-bodied sailors in 1931 were given $25 a month aboard the Finnish-owned ships, and the ordinaries hardly received enough to buy the seaboots, sweaters and oilskins needed for Cape Horn, and a few cans of Copenhagen snuff. Some of the boys got nothing at all, and others even paid for their training. Many were Germans who, according to the owner, were lucky to find a berth and the training no longer available at home. The same thing was true for the British apprentices, but the British were older, most had some sea experience and could qualify as able-bodied sailors and perform the difficult work aloft.

The Cape Horn road turned out a hard-bitten breed of youngsters. Two ordinary seamen, named Finila and Beckman, who served in the big, heavy *Grace Harwar,* were typical. By the time they were seventeen, both had sailed twice around Cape Horn, and had logged 100,000 miles at sea. They knew the main ports and most of the outports, including the guano islands off the Peruvian coast and in the Indian Ocean; and the Puget Sound reaches where, inside the log boom, there was only a sawmill and a dock; and the drab coastal towns of New South Wales where wheat was loaded, sack by sack.

When they went home, they were tattooed. They wore wooden-pegged leather seaboots, chewed snuff, and swaggered. The land wasn't for them; as quickly as they could, they returned to sea.

Conditions aboard the Cape Horners were so bad in the early 1930's, they foretold the fate of all square-rigged ships. It took either boyish bravado or intense economic need to sign articles in the vessels that were left. These were big, hard-working ships. When they had been built they carried an average crew of forty men. Now the crews were down to thirteen, and twelve, and all of them boys.

Herzogin Cecilie, the particular pride and joy of Gustaf Erikson, the shrewd Åland Island owner of the last square-rigged fleet, had been designed as a training ship to be handled by a crew of from forty to 100 boys. When she was under the Erikson house flag at the end of her career, her crew mustered twenty-six.

Captain Erikson understood every phase of the problem. He was aware that in the old days of sail, a crack clipper like the famous British *Cutty Sark* of 963 tons carried more than thirty-five hands. Other clippers, the East Indiamen, and the Blackball frigates, and the packet ships had been manned by more than fifty sailors.

But sailing ships could no longer afford to carry full crews. In the 1930's the average steamer cargo discharge rate was 500 tons a day. With her relatively clumsy gear, a sailing ship could unload only a fraction as much cargo, possibly 100 tons. A steamer's insurance rate was ten percent of her worth, that of a sailing ship 55 percent.

This forced sailing ships to accept lower freight rates than steamers, or retire from the seas. Erikson, in close touch with international shipping conditions, bought

Captain Gustav Erikson of Marie-hamn, Finland, collected most of the remnants of the international square-rigger fleet. The three-masted steel bark *Penang* served in the Erikson fleet from 1923, when it was first purchased, until 1941, when it was lost with all on board.

151

up one by one the old square-riggers which he believed he could operate at a profit; and he sailed them everywhere in the world.

The four-mast bark *Herzogin Cecilie* had belonged to the North German Lloyd, and he bought other German vessels, some from the famous Laeiz Line, some from the British and some from the French. Eventually he assembled a fleet of twenty based on the little Åland Island port of Mariehamn, off Finland. His purchase price in the lean shipping years after World War I went as low as $20,000 for a vessel.

Erikson had come gradually to the status of shipowner. He was a native of Lemmland, near Mariehamn, and went to sea at the age of nine as ship's cook. Then, at fourteen, he qualified as able-bodied sailor, was bosun at seventeen, mate at eighteen, and master in a North Sea Trader at nineteen. All of his time was spent in sailing ships, and when he came ashore to operate as an owner he believed implicitly in the use of boys for the crews, and young mates, and masters.

He often sent out his ships in ballast to Australia, willing to take the gamble on the profit he might make months later from wheat cargoes. Around 1930, the average freight charge for Australian grain was $7.50 a ton. *Herzogin Cecilie,* one of the biggest ships, took 5,000 tons in cargo. This brought Erikson $37,500. But he had to pay for the outward-bound ballast run, and tug charges, and brokerage, and pilotage charges, harbor dues, port dues, insurance, lighterage, stevedores, and food, and wages, and canvas. Food and wages never came to much in an Erikson ship, but new canvas could cost as high as $2,500 for a single voyage. Erikson shaved his expense list very fine, holding long talks with his masters about what they spent while their vessels were in foreign ports.

The four-masted bark *Lawhill* sailed in the Calcutta jute trade for many years. She was dismasted in 1904 during a typhoon, and once took 190 days from Philadelphia to Chittagong. She became part of the Erikson fleet in 1919.

Five-masted schooner *Cap Nord* is towed to sea from port Bristol, England. The vessel was built in 1918 at North Vancouver, British Columbia.

Still, even with the most careful management, the Erikson Line would not have stayed in business if the owner had conducted it in the usual way. Captain Erikson had three outstanding factors that helped him succeed. His company did not pay insurance; it had no overhead; and there was no depreciation. He was his own manager, his own marine superintendent, and his own board of directors. He lived in a wooden house beside the dirt main street of Mariehamn, and his office was a hut out in the garden.

Captain Erikson was really a one-man company. He studied, accepted or rejected the risks involved, and made all the decisions regarding the operation of the ships. There could be no depreciation of their value because he bought the ships when their owners had withdrawn from square-rigger competition. The prices he had paid were so little above the scrap value that, as long as the vessels remained afloat, they could never be worth less than their purchase sums.

There were in the early 1930's more than twenty square-rigged ships that annually hauled wheat from St. Vincent's Gulf or Spencer Gulf in Australia to English Channel ports. Fourteen of the seventeen Finnish ships in this trade belonged to Erikson. His masters, mates and petty officers were Swedish-speaking, but Finnish nationals. They respected him, his knowledge of ship-handling and his business acumen.

It was the focsle hands who complained about the Erikson Line ships, and with reason.

Aerial view of the harbor at Mariehamn, the only city on the Aland Islands. It was from here th

...ptain Gustav Erikson operated his fleet of sailing ships, dealing mainly in the Australian grain trade.

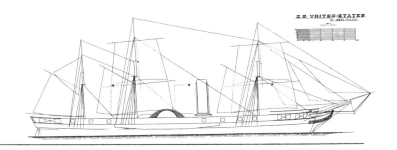

CHAPTER FIFTEEN

The Hardship School

... there was no fresh water, and men labored aloft thirsty, weak with hunger.

THE OLD, PROUD, spirit was gone, and men lived meanly aboard ship in common focsles with low overheads, crude toilets, bunks jammed one against the other. Food was brought from the galley aft in messkids, often cold when it arrived in the focsle, and seldom enough. Washing was done out of buckets, the fresh water strictly rationed. A sailor was supplied with a bare bunk, a place on the mess bench, and if he were in a "good ship," space for his oilskins and sea chest.

Some of the voyages at the end of the square-rigger days took the ships three times around the world in the weary search for cargo. They loaded guano, or coal, or rock salt, or a few hundred sacks of wheat. The ships lay for months in the outports, empty, or in ballast, waiting for orders. The crews, without money and unable to get ashore, came to hate each other, the ship, the sea. There were savage fights in the cramped focsle living space and out on deck. Men said that they would be glad to see Cape Horn again; at least they would be headed back toward Europe and home.

Food aboard the last of the square-riggers was just above the subsistence level. It was salt meat, either beef or pork, dried fish, peas and beans. Potatoes were part of the diet until they disappeared, and several live pigs were kept on the main deck, slaughtered at intervals by one of the sailors who had been appointed butcher by the mate. Coffee, tea, milk, sugar and salt were issued according to regulations under the British Board of Trade Act of 1906, a copy of which, carefully framed, hung on the bulkhead in every focsle. It was the owner who put it there, not the crew, but often sailors had to cite parts to the steward or the captain because of violations.

Deck scene aboard the bark *Manunui* of Sidney, Australia, as the watch goes aloft to shorten sail. Conditions for seamen grew steadily worse and the work became both more difficult and dangerous. When the *Manunui* was wrecked in 1915, some of the men shown here went down with her.

A sailor brought into the ship with him his own mess gear, knife, fork and spoon, in the same fashion as his bunk gear, his straw mattress and his blankets. He understood his rights under the law, but a man who protested too much came to be called a "sea lawyer," and the mates soon singled him out for special treatment. He was sent aloft a great deal, or on a dark night was knocked down from behind by a marline spike blow, kicked in the ribs, face and backside until he could hardly stagger forward to his bunk.

Food was important on a ship, but discipline came first, and nearly all "sea lawyers" learned discretion. They and the rest of their hungry focsle mates had to use their wits to get an extra meal. Sometimes they pounded up hard sea biscuit with a belaying pin and when the steward was below, they begged or stole a little molasses from the cook. With the connivance of the cook, they put the messy concoction in the galley stove. It was a rare treat for the men.

The daily diet was pea soup, salt beef, an occasional piece of salt pork, and, for Sunday dinner, "preserved" beef. Breakfast was "burgoo"—a watery porridge that in most of the ships contained a strong flavor of crushed weevils. Supper was whatever a man could save from his noon meal, or his breakfast; more times than not, he went without anything except a chew of snuff.

A square-rigger's daily work routine was almost incredibly hard compared with modern standards. Men worked in four hour watches, and more when they were needed to tack ship. When there was extra work, the members of the watch below whose turn it was to rest, were called on deck by a sharp rap of a marline spike on the focsle door and the shout, "All hands!"

Setting the main topsail as the *Governor Goodwin* slips out of Boston in August, 1891. Five years later the ship was wrecked on Princes Island.

The Captain and the owner of the *Governor Goodwin* survey Boston harbor from the topside of the deckhouse just before sailing.

Bohemia of San Francisco, California, was built in 1875 at Bath, Maine. The ship was bought and reconditioned by Cecil B. deMille, for use in his motion pictures. Experienced seamen were hired to work aloft.

In fair weather the mate checked the ship at dawn before the new watch was called. There were always some duties to be performed, and he pointed them out to the sleepy-eyed, stumbling sailors. Braces were hauled, sheets trimmed, and, grunting, men grasped the main royal halyard and sweated the yard a few inches higher until the mate nodded and called, "Belay." Then they could have their morning coffee.

The man at the wheel, standing his one hour trick, was just as eager as the rest for his coffee. He rang three bells smartly on the ship's bell, watched the cook come out of the galley door with the big, black pot. After coffee-time the ship was pumped, and after breakfast the day's long routine began.

The salt water hose was rigged. Sand was sprinkled on deck and the holy stones shunted back and forth until the deck planks were spotless; around the bulwarks and the bitts and the fish plates, sand and canvas were used. When the mate was content with the condition of the deck, chipping hammers and scrapers were applied to old paint; lamps were trimmed; sailors, who had the skill, gave a hand to the sail maker; others, who took great pride in their work, went aloft to renew gear, set up a block or serve off a sail earring worn thin.

Storm dominated the thoughts of nearly all the younger members of the crews. They had heard of the casualties in the other ships. When storm conditions prevailed, they worked right down in the waist of the ship on the main deck, straining with every bit of strength to swing around the huge steel yard that supported the 100-foot wide and 40-foot deep mainsail. They hauled waist-deep, sometimes shoulder-deep,

As the Danish barkentine *Laura* heads for the open sea in chilly weather, two sailors go out to work on the outer jib. The land mass merges into the horizon astern, the ship moves ahead under full sails. Her useful years over, the *Laura* was converted to a hulk in 1924.

in a welter of water; if they let go the brace when a wave came slamming aboard, the ship might dismast herself, and so they hung on, and ducked their heads, and felt the tons of water tearing at them.

Some of the ships had no protection aft for the wheelsman. That was how the two boys were lost from the *Killoran*. They clung to the wheel spokes as long as they could, and then, as a giant wave swept them away, they probably screamed. But no one heard; and it was only when the rudder kicked violently and the ship almost broached that the rest of the crew knew the pair were gone.

Better-kept ships, back in the prosperous days, were equipped with sturdy structures at the stern that gave safety to the wheelsman. These were built of wood, or steel, and raised between him and the taffrail. It was well known that a sailing vessel taking seas over her stern could not live long. She would roll so deeply with the weight of water taken aboard that waves would cross her from either side. Then she would sink, and very fast. Still, there were shipowners who refused to build such stern structures. They called them "dog-houses" and said that in the old times a man steered the ship in the open, in any kind of weather.

Herzogin Cecilie was caught in a storm once when all hands were needed to handle her gear and furl sail. One of the crew—a boy named Ringe—was left alone at the wheel. He steered the bulky ship until his strength gave out. He hung on desperately on the spokes of the big double wheel, head-high to him, his feet braced hard and wide on the steering platform. Suddenly a wave, bigger than the others, came up astern and smashed against the rudder. The shock travelled upward through the rudder stock and the steering gear to the wheel and Ringe's tight hands.

Two views of the *Herzogin Cecilie,* Bremerhaven-built bark of the Erikson fleet. She rides close offshore, waiting for wind until at last, the wind-jammer is under way with a brisk breeze from the starboard quarter.

161

The spin of the wheel pitched the boy up and over. He came down on his head and shoulders, smashed against the deck and wrenched his foot as he tumbled over. The ship lunged wildly through the storm in total darkness. Spindrift shot across the poop in blinding sheets and Ringe could not see the main deck only a few feet from him. He called for help several times before he realized that none of the men could hear him. No one saw what had happened.

Ringe crawled back to the wheel. He got to his feet and braced himself, chose the exact instant when, under the thrust of her remaining canvas, the wind and the waves upon her, she eased a bit. Then he groped for the slick, fast-jerking wheel spokes, grasped them, and steadied the ship. *Herzogin Cecilie* came safely out of the storm.

There are many other stories of brave, desperate boys who saved their vessels or their shipmates in times of great danger. Still, the daring they displayed arose from sheer necessity. There was no excitement left for them in the so-called "Grain Race" around Cape Horn. There were only so many girls at home who would gape at wooden-pegged seaboots and China-side style tattoos. Boys became men rapidly in the last of the square-riggers, and few of the older ones remained. They went into steamers, or they went ashore. Romance, they told their younger shipmates, didn't count at the pay table.

The story of Ronald Walker is one of the most poignant examples of the fascination the Cape Horn run had for young men. And his death showed in stark detail the needless dangers present during a voyage in the last of the square-rigger era.

Walker was a young Australian newspaper reporter and yachtsman. He and his friend, Alan J. Villiers, joined the full-rigged ship *Grace Harwar* as seamen. They planned to make a movie of a square-rigger rounding Cape Horn, a trip whose dangers dominated the modern folklore of the sea.

Grace Harwar was a 1,760 ton Clyde-built ship, forty years old at the time, and not in the best of shape. When they boarded her they noticed immediately the absence of any labor-saving devices. Dangerous conditions were apparent: the steering wheel was exposed and, aloft, some of the footropes were badly rusted and obviously treacherous.

But Walker and Villiers were determined to see their adventure through and sailed with the ship when she left South Australia on April 17, 1929. They were prepared to accept all the dangers, and knew they were heading for Cape Horn in a season of bitter Antarctic winter gales. The crew was much too small and untrained to handle the ship except when all hands were on deck.

There were four Australians in the crew, an Englishman, a Frenchman, and the rest were Swedish-speaking Finns who came from the Åland Islands. For the Finns it was their first voyage, and all were young boys, and some were deserters from other ships anxious to get home. Three of the focsle lot had never been to sea before in any capacity. The average age on board the ship was around nineteen.

Passat, part of the Erikson fleet from 1932 until she was sold to Belgium in 1952. A four-masted steel bark, the *Passat* worked mainly in the Australian grain trade.

Grace Harwar, the Erikson square-rigger on which Alan Villiers sailed as an able-bodied sailor long before he became internationally known both as author and shipmaster.

163

Grace Harwar met storm at sea right after she cleared land and stood on her Cape Horn course. The mizzen topgallantsail blew out during the first night. There was nothing ready to replace it. A new one must be sewn by hand and on deck. It would have to wait until the weather cleared.

High, heavy seas coming aboard kept the focsle door shut. If it remained open, the watch below might drown, be swept on deck, or flung overside. With the door shut, the focsle smell was unbearable. All hands were soaked and lacked dry clothing. There was no heat in the place. Men flopped, seaboots, oilskins and all, into the shallow wooden bunks. Their bodies were covered with sea boils inside their clothing; their hands were raw from dragging at wire, wet canvas and rope. Sleepless, they stared up at the bulkheads where moisture formed and dripped unchecked, and moss had begun to grow. It was so cold the cockroaches and the bedbugs had crawled away to hide.

For days, the galley fire was out because of the seas that breasted aboard. The watches stumbled hungry to work, seven in one, six in the other, both needed on deck when the ship was tacked. Coffee was a nagging dream, like food, but, worse, there was no fresh water, and men labored aloft thirsty, weak with hunger. When they looked down from the yards, they could see the fresh water pump as it emerged from the recoil of a wave. Not long enough, though, they knew, for them to use it. The pump was old, worn, not much good; sea water might mix through the intake and pollute what fresh water was left in the tank.

The thirty-eighth day at sea, in storm and approaching Cape Horn, at four o'clock in the morning, the captain decided to break out the fore upper topgallantsail. Ronald Walker and a small Finnish boy were ordered aloft to loosen canvas so that the sail could be hoisted. Walker and the boy obeyed. Down on deck, the other five members of the watch, with the second mate helping, began to haul up the halyards.

Then the weather clew of the sail fouled in the gear. The second mate bawled aloft to Walker to clear it. Walker moved out on the lower topgallant yard and released the clew. The men on deck hauled again, hoisting both sail and upper topgallant yard. Perhaps Walker, still crouching on the yard, heard the sharp sound as the halyards parted under the strain. But he had no chance to get out of the way. The steel yard came hurtling down to crush him in a tangle of rigging.

Villiers, working on deck, stared upward, realizing his friend was badly hurt. He leaped to the ratlines, up he went and out onto the footrope, along the yard, and reached the limp body. He shouted in the storm but Walker did not answer. Then, fearing the worst, Villiers signalled to the deck for help. A gantline was reeved and sent up to him and he lowered his friend's still body tenderly, very slowly, carefully. As he returned to the deck, Villiers still believed that his friend might be alive. It was the Captain who told him.

Walker was buried from the poop deck the next day with all the traditional

The *Ben Venue* was one of the best of the steel-hulled ships built in the Clydeside yards of Scotland. But in 1882 both the *Ben Venue* and the *City of Perth* were beached by a typhoon in Caroline Bay, Timaru.

ceremony of a sea burial. The second mate, who took responsibility for the accident, went around blaming himself for the young man's death. *Grace Harwar* drove on for Cape Horn through continuous storms, and the mate gradually went insane.

As the voyage continued, water began to seep into the ship through openings around the hatches, through companionways where the planks had worked loose, and through the deck seams, washed open by the action of countless seas. The pumps jammed and the sodden ship wallowed heavily.

The crew could do nothing. They huddled together on the poop. It snowed, and the whiteness blanked the great, roaring wastes of water. There was just the ship, bound somehow for Falmouth with a cargo of wheat, an old, rusty prison, a symbol of the end.

"Channel fever," the seamen's term for impatience to leave the ship, has caught the crew of this unidentified square-rigger. Dressed in their best, they are preparing to go ashore.

Handsome wooden-hulled *Laima*, one of the last of her kind, used in the coastal trade.

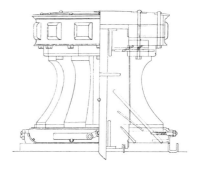

CHAPTER SIXTEEN

Twilight Darkens

. . . ten rusty square-riggers through which the rats scampered.

WHEN THE LAST OF THE European sailing fleet went to the shipbreakers after World War II, square-rigged vessels had all but disappeared from the sea. The really great American ships, the record-breaking clippers, had long since faded into history. They had been sunk, wrecked, beached as a total loss, or gone missing, or had burned, or, even worse, at the end had been cut down to nameless barges and scows.

The same was true for the famous British ships of the halcyon clipper days. *Thermopylae,* and *Cedric the Saxon,* and *Salamis,* and *Titania,* and their proud sisters had gone into limbo. A stubborn-minded group of British citizens who believed in the historic value of *Cutty Sark* had saved her, and that was all.

American shipowners had given up many years before World War II any attempt to operate square-riggers on a commercial basis. Along the Pacific Coast, in the backwaters of San Francisco Bay, anchored in Sausalito and moored in Alameda, there were ten rusty square-riggers through which the rats scampered. A full-rigged wooden ship lay desolate in San Pedro while big tanker vessels steamed past into Terminal Island, loaded, and were sent out again in a few hours. Up in Winslow, in the State of Washington, two four-mast barks, *Mosholu* and *Monongohela,* had been idle for years.

The record of the wanderings of *Mosholu* before she came to her final berth is typical of many of the fine old ships. She was built by W. Hamilton & Company in Glasgow, Scotland, in 1904, and then sold to a German firm. Following the peace terms of World War I, she was handed over to the United States as part of a war reparations payment.

Captain Gustav Erikson of Mariehamn bought her in 1935 and put her in the Australian trade under Captain Gunnar Boman. She remained quite active, and was well-known in the Cape Horn fleet. But during World War II she was caught by the Germans when she put into Narvik, Norway, with a cargo of linseed oil. Her Finnish captain still aboard, she served the Nazis as a depot ship. The Russians seized her when the Germans retreated from Norway, and finally she got back to her owners.

Her owners sold the ship at a low price, seeing little future for her, and they were right. She made only a very few more voyages before she was left at her Winslow berth in rusty ruin.

Perhaps fate was kinder to some of her sister ships of the Erikson fleet. The famous *Olivebank,* bound for the Baltic in 1939, hit a mine and sank fast. Seven men of her crew who managed to cling to her mast-heads were saved by a Danish fishing boat.

The *Penang,* formerly named *Albert Rickmers,* had remained until 1941 in New Zealand waters where she safely traded. Then she was sent to Europe with a cargo of Australian grain. An Italian submarine got her. Seventeen of her crew were lost.

These ships were the last square-riggers kept in active service. There was no more work for their kind. The owners of commercial ships were finished with sail as a means of motive power except in inland waters and for very limited coastwise work. Vessels that had been rigged in essentially the same way for over 450 years, and which had been used by all the great circumnavigators of history, were about to go out of existence forever.

The huge, 5,000-ton steel bark *Moshulu* was built in Glasgow, Scotland, for a German shipping line in 1904. Given to the United States as part of World War I reparations, it eventually was sold to Captain Erikson and used primarily in the Australian trade. *Moshulu* was the last and largest of the Erikson ships.

Forgotten and left to rust in Oakland Estuary are *John Ena, Lasbek, Mae Dollar,* and *John Rolph.* Photographed on December 18, 1927.

The remnants of the sailing ship fleet that Robert S. Dollar had gathered after World War I were left untended, abandoned in remote Puget Sound anchorages. The largest collection of square-riggers under American registery was owned by the Alaska Packers Company. It lay in basin at Oakland, California, in what had come to be known as Rotten Row. The ships' yards hung askew. Running rigging was gone. Standing rigging was about to go. No attempt was made at ship-keeping or repair. The vessels were really worthless.

Hollywood film producers raised a bit of hope when they picked up a couple of ships from total decay. They rebuilt old square-riggers to look like HMS *Bounty,* and *Pandora,* and the ship from which "Billy Budd" was taken, *Rights of Man.* But the needs of the movie industry were small and did not last long. Men who could rig and handle sailing vessels drifted away from the ports and left the sea either in retirement or disgust.

Some East Coast schooners had been kept in operation, on a very narrow margin of profit, until the 1942-5 war years. But the owners were soon afterwards forced out of business. Steamer competition badly hurt the schooner trade, and then long haul trucks that used the coastal highways finished it. The vessels found various fates. None of them was quite as strange, though, as those suffered by others already sold for what the market would bring.

A pair of old schooners serving out their last days as protection for a pylon of the Carquinez Bridge in San Francisco Bay. The *Bangor* still had her masts in 1931, but the *Caroline* had been stripped and her hull used as a barge.

Abner Coburn (left) beached and set on fire to salvage the metals in her.

The hulk of the wooden-hulled *Fairhaven*, once a proud schooner that sailed out of Fairhaven, Massachusetts.

A number of them had finished on Rum Row in the violent, brutal period of Prohibition. They had been rammed by launches filled with hijackers. Their deckhouses bore bullet holes from fusillades and warning volleys fired by Coast Guardsmen in close pursuit. Others had pitched through winter gales at anchor while the entire crew lay sodden-drunk below, and in the night passenger liners sounded whistle blasts and steered clear just in time.

Some, on both the East and West coasts, served briefly as gambling "clubs" offshore. They were raided either by the police or by gangsters, and the vessels returned to their backwater berths. One, *Jacob A. Stambler,* became a dockside hotel. Another, *Cora F. Cressy,* a big cargo-hauler, was rebuilt as a honky-tonky night club, and after that was used as a lobster pound.

Most of the ships stayed at their berths, beyond repair or hope of future use. Their seams slowly opened. Planks and timbers gave, and gradually the vessels settled, listing a bit more each year. Their topsides and cabins were stripped of anything worthwhile. The masts stood naked, shrouds, halyards, gaffs and booms gone. A thick green scum marked the high tide mark, and on the bowsprit gulls perched and flapped their wings.

Morning Star of New Bedford, Massachusetts, a missionary ship, under sail. Built in 1853, she was lost at sea May 10, 1918. (Below) A whaling ship hove down for coppering.

171

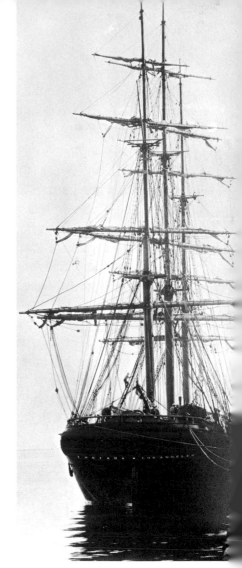

Strange were the final uses of surviving sailing ships. The *Rights of Man*, with a figurehead of a freed slave, was used in the movie "Billy Budd." The wooden hulled *Indiana* was bought by Cecil B. de Mille from the Alaska Packers Association and continually remodeled for various motion pictures.

The men who had formed the sailing ship crews were slow to die. They belonged to a hardy breed. But Sailors' Snug Harbor in New York City and the British Seamen's Home and similar institutions on the Continent marked the losses each year. Here, the last man to sail a clipper was gone. There, no more square-rigger veterans were left. And even former schooner sailors were becoming rare.

Along the docksides in the United States, and in the British ports, and in the North Seas and Baltic and Scandinavian harbor towns, where in the old days the sailing ships had crowded, the deepwater men got together. They talked of Cape Horn in the winter gales, and of all the hazards they had survived under sail. But the tradition of the wind-driven ships was dying, the old sailors knew. It would be forgotten once they were gone.

Profound sadness filled their talk. Twilight for the sailing ships meant more than the loss of jobs for a few thousand men. It foretold the end of a way of life that reached back beyond the beginnings of history.

There were still some sail-rigged coasters around the British Isles. Bright-hulled feluccas with lateen sails put out after fish from the Spanish and Portuguese ports and from Italian harbors in the Mediterranean. Small, locally built schooners hauled cargo between the Caribbean islands, and junks and sampans and dhows ran among the Philippines and in the China Seas and the Arabian Gulf. Bugeyes and skipjacks and oyster bateaux were used in the wide waters of Chesapeake Bay; and on up the eastern American coast, in Long Island Sound, in the Maine fishing towns and in Canada, a few sloops were kept in commission.

That was about all, if a man didn't count the sailing yachts. More of those were being built each year, and some countries still maintained square-rigged vessels for the training of their naval and merchant marine cadets. There were not many training vessels, though, and shipbuilders' plans went beyond steam and diesels to atomic power. Wind-ships belonged almost completely to the past.

The brig *Carnegie* was built in Brooklyn, New York for the Carnegie Institute and used as a laboratory for scientific work.

The bark *Jacob A. Stambler* was converted into a dockside hotel by the Arbuckle Deep Sea Hotel Company and tied at an East River pier, only to burn there in 1916.

The five-masted auxiliary schooner *Cora F. Cressy* was built in Bath, Maine, in 1902, with a fine, raked bow and long bowsprit. To serve the coastwise trade, she was not equipped with steam power. That is a tugboat, alongside on her starboard quarter. The fine ship was obsolete before her maiden voyage—technology had passed her by. After several profitless years, the *Cora F. Cressy* was warped alongside a dock in New Haven, Connecticut, and turned into a cheap showboat. The venture, however, was not successful. The old ship was forgotten until 1938 when she was towed out to sea for burning. But somehow the plans were changed at the last minute. She was not burned. In 1952 the *Cora F. Cressy* was discovered in Keene's Neck, Muscongus Bay, Maine, serving her owners as a lobster pound.

THE WHITE HOUSE

WASHINGTON

From my first race on Nantucket Sound many years
ago to my most recent outing as a weekend sailor,
sailing has given me some of the most pleasant and
exciting moments of my life. It also has taught me
something of the courage, resourcefulness and strength
required of men who sail the seas in ships. Thus, I
am looking forward eagerly to Operation Sail. The
sight of so many ships gathered from the distant corners
of the world should remind us that strong, disciplined
and venturesome men still can find their way safely
across uncertain and stormy seas.

John F. Kennedy

THE WHITE HOUSE

WASHINGTON

I know that President Kennedy had a
deep and personal interest in "Operation
Sail." Both in memory of our late President
and because I share his admiration for men
who sail the seas in ships, I am happy to
continue the encouragement he gave to this
international effort.

Operation Sail, 1964 *Rotterdam* looms above the bow of the *Christian Radich*   Photo by Michael Chassid

The graceful Portuguese training bark *Sagres* sailing past the Statue of Liberty in New York harbor during the final review of Operation Sail, 1964.

Norwegian training ship *Staatsraad Lemkuhl* about to pass under the new Verrazano Bridge, which links Brooklyn with Staten Island across The Narrows.

"The sail-by in New York harbor..."
Brigantine *St. Lawrence II* of Canada (*above, left*) and the full-rigged ship *Danmark* of Denmark (*above, right*). Full-rigged ship *Libertad* of Argentina (*bottom, left*) Schooner *Juan Sebastian de Elcano* of Spain (*right*).

Photos by Jeff Blinn

THE
MAIN PARTS
OF A
FULL-RIGGED
SHIP

1. BOWSPRIT
2. JIB BOOM
3. BOBSTAYS
4. MARTINGALE
   (DOLPHIN
   STRIKER)
5. BOW
6. STERN
7. RUDDER

8. FOREMAST
8A. FORE SAIL
8B. LOWER FORE-
    TOPSAIL
8C. UPPER FORE-
    TOPSAIL
8D. FORE-TOP-
    GALLANT SAIL
8E. FOREROYAL
8F. FORE SKYSAIL
8G. FORE MAST
8H. FORE-TOPMAST
8I. FOREROYAL
    MAST

9. MAINMAST
9A. MAINSAIL
9B. LOWER MAIN
    TOPSAIL
9C. UPPER MAIN TOPSAIL
9D. MAIN TOPGALLANT
9E. MAIN ROYAL
9F. MAIN SKYSAIL
9G. MAINMAST
9H. MAIN TOPMAST
9I. MAIN-ROYAL MAST

"Past the mid-point of the 19th century..."   Clipper ship *Shakespeare*   Painting by William York

"And a century later..."   Barkentine *Esmeralda* of Chile   Photograph by Jeff Blinn

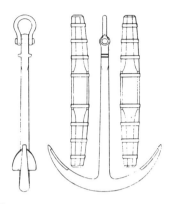

CHAPTER SEVENTEEN

Operation Sail

. . . I share his admiration for the men who sail the sea in ships—

PRESIDENT LYNDON B. JOHNSON

THE NEEDS OF INTERNATIONAL COMMERCE changed drastically after World War II, and with them the ships that carried the cargoes and the greatly increased number of passengers. The new vessels were highly powered, designed to make consistently fast voyages. But the sea forces were the same, the mysterious and tremendous winds, the tides and currents which in combination or alone could take any vessel from her course, make her a total, foundering wreck.

So the old virtues of sailing ship work were still valuable, and should be practiced, studied and understood by modern seamen. They could be learned in only one way, by sending young cadet officers to sea for several months a year in square-rigged ships.

A young man sent aloft in the middle of a black night to fist in and secure salt-stiff canvas more than 150 feet above the deck would later be extremely sensitive to the effects of the wind. He would also, when he came to officer rank, observe with great care the steering of his vessel in unusual weather and tidal and current circumstances. Long hours at the wheel of a square-rigger while she lay hardly moving in light airs, or in gale conditions when she ran under lower topsails, her lee rail awash, would leave him with a keen sense of ship handling. He would use radar to watch the horizon, and loran to find the ship's position by means of radio beams, and all the other electronic devices aboard the modern vessel where he served. But, first and last, he would trust his own responses to the problems of the sea, and his sense of judgment, alert ever since his cadet training in sail.

The host ship to the visiting sailing fleet, the United States Coast Guard bark *Eagle* drops anchor in the Hudson River, off Riverside Drive.

The history of both World Wars gave validity to the theory of sailing ship training. Thousands of men needlessly lost their lives when ships had been abandoned and the crews had taken to the lifeboats. Basic sea knowledge was lacking—how to rig a mainsail and a jib, how to handle them, then navigate with a small compass through storms and calms, catch fish, catch birds, and rain water. The sea was alien for these men who were lost; it was an enemy, and not a friend.

Much more was involved in the sail training theory than war-time survival. During a man's career at sea in peace aboard a modern vessel, he might only for the space of a few minutes have to concentrate all that he had learned. Then he would hold his ship from a fatal collision course in fog, or he would ease her down-wind towards a vessel in distress, protecting the lifeboat that took off survivors.

Automation was of little good in such emergencies, and speed was in itself a form of danger. Ship collisions and serious accidents still occurred.

But the great fleets of sailing ships were gone now, and with them went a way of life that had raised generations of master seamen. The awesome beauty of a harbor crowded with tall masts was a rare memory.

The full-rigged Norwegian training ship *Christian Radich*, sunlight bright on her sails, catches the wind as she enters the Upper Bay.

West Germany's bark *Gorch Fock II* clearing lower Manhattan with tugs accompanying her. (Right) Cadets aboard the ship go up the ratlines in their dress uniforms.

There were skipjacks and bugeyes and oyster sloops in service in Chesapeake Bay, but they were small craft, and never went offshore. A few schooners began to make a living for their owners in the 1940's and '50's in Maine waters, and around Cape Cod and Martha's Vineyard, and along the East Coast of Florida. They were advertised as "wind-jammers", and attracted people who were pleased to cruise under sail and willing to pay for it. The sailing cruise business has increased recently, and is doing very well in the Bahamas and some of the other British West Indian islands, Antigua in particular. A fleet of big former yachts, ketches and yawls is operated from Antigua, and extensive cruises are made through the islands during the winter months.

Work schooners are still found in the Caribbean. They serve as fishermen out of Bahamian, Jamaican, Haitian and Dominican ports, and as general cargo carriers between the smaller islands right on down to the coast of Venezuela. Their skillfully patched sails—"a patch on a patch, that's us, mon"—their hand-hewn hull planks and pole masts form a familiar silhouette in all of the island harbors, and they will continue to operate for a long time to come. The West Indians are more than excellent sailors; they build their own craft, load and discharge them, and know how to keep costs and cargo rates low.

There were in the Port of New York and along the East coast of the United States a small group of men who determined that the sailing ship tradition should live. They were all of them sailors or men who had for years been in active, intimate contact with the sea. It was not their intention to quarrel with the use of atomic power or any other new means of ship propulsion.

With all her canvas spread, the Danish ship *Danmark* sails into the harbor, as the Statue of Liberty holds her welcome torch in the distance.

The sleek yawl *Tawau*, which had participated in the Newport-to-Bermuda race, carried the British ensign in the harbor ceremonies.

They cited the fine record of the United States Coast Guard bark *Eagle* as a training ship for cadets. The example of the *Eagle* and the sail training given by various nations could be used to revive public interest in square-rigged ships. This could help insure a broad and lasting program of training future officers in wind driven vessels.

There was already a strong upsurge in small craft sailing at the American maritime cadet academies. Annapolis was first, as the beneficiary of some fine ocean-going yachts, to take part in the bi-annual Newport-Bermuda race. The United States Merchant Marine Academy and the Maritime College of New York State University later entered the event, and with them the Coast Guard Academy.

Eight boats from the service academies were in the 1964 race, and *Icefire,* a 45-foot yawl representing the United States Merchant Marine Academy, came in best among them. She was awarded the Atlantic Destroyer Trophy for this. When she returned to her home berth alongside the academy dock at Kings Point, Long Island, she was flying a broom at her mast-head, the ancient signal of victory at sea.

Other nations, too, used sailing ships for cadet training. But the ships were scattered in distant ports all over the world.

A plan to bring together as many of the remaining old ships slowly began to form. The idea had begun with Nils Hansel, an ardent yachtsman. He had passed it on to Commodore John S. Baylis, United States Coast Guard, Retired.

Commodore Baylis was a graduate of the New York Nautical Schoolship *St. Marys* and of the Coast Guard Academy. He had made four European cruises on the square-rigged *St. Marys,* and a circumnavigation voyage as a member of the crew

190

The *Dewarutji* came from Indonesia to take part in Operation Sail. In the background are Grant's Tomb and the Riverside Church.

Sorlandet, one of the three Norwegian ships that crossed the Atlantic to take part in Operation Sail, moves slowly up the Hudson River.

of the British four-masted bark *Arrow,* and served for three Arctic voyages aboard the Revenue Cutter *Bear.*

The third to join in the plan was Frank O. Braynard of the Moran Towing and Transportation Company, a marine historian.

The group gradually gathered support, and formed a committee, Operation Sail. It received the enthusiastic endorsement of President John F. Kennedy. The Sail Training Association, a British organization that sponsored a square-rigger race from Lisbon to Bermuda, also offered its cooperation.

A call went out to all the maritime nations of the world, inviting them to send their sailing ships—now used for cadet training—to New York.

Operation Sail became a continuation of the 1964 Lisbon-Bermuda race. Eight square-rigged ships and four smaller fore-and-afters participated during June, 1964 in the Lisbon-Bermuda race. While the contestants lay over in Hamilton harbor, they were joined by three more square-riggers, the Coast Guard bark *Eagle,* the Chilean Navy barkentine *Esmeralda,* and the Indonesian barkentine *Dewarutji.* The tall ships then sailed from Bermuda in company with the smaller craft, and made the passage mostly in light airs to Gravesend Bay at the entrance of New York harbor.

The formal review of Operation Sail was held July 14, 1964 in New York harbor. Secretary of the Navy Paul Nitze represented President Johnson, and reviewed the sailing fleet from the aircraft carrier USS *Randolph.* The sail-by had grown to more than twenty vessels from a dozen nations. Navy destroyers and Coast Guard craft flanked the fairway that led from the lower bay under the Verrazano-Narrows Bridge past the *Randolph* and toward Manhattan and moorings in the Hudson River.

Dawn on the morning of July 14 was thick with fog. There had been rain squalls, but no wind stirred. Now, suddenly, at the exact time of review, sunlight blazed over the upper bay, and into it from seaward came the tall ships, the vast, shadowy arc of the bridge above them.

Eagle led the column formed by the square-riggers. Her immaculate white hull gleamed with the luster of pearl shell. When she was abeam of *Randolph* and had dipped her ensign in salute, she unfurled and sheeted home her sails. The ships astern of her followed her action. The Portuguese ship *Sagres* spread sails that bore the blazoned red insignia of the Cross of Jesus. The handsome Norwegian full-rigged ship *Christian Radich,* which had won the Lisbon-Bermuda race, sent her cadets sprinting around the deck capstans as her yards were braced.

Ship followed ship, majestically, until they had all passed in review and were secured at their Hudson River moorings. More than a century had been thrust aside. Moving out of the mist with the tall ships were long-remembered names, Columbus, Magellan, and Drake, Palmer, Cressy. Those had been great captains, and were still.

The beauty of the fleet brought back the famous names. But Robert Fulton, whose crude little steamer *Clermont* had navigated this same stretch of river and created the first twilight of the sailing ships, was not remembered on this day.

Training of Future Officers

Today the last of the great wind-driven vessels are maintained chiefly as schools for future officers of the Merchant Marine. Most of the world's maritime nations have a deep appreciation of the lifelong skills gained by training aboard sailing ships.

"The sense and feel of the sea"—compounded of strength of character, courage and determination, cool alertness, an understanding of the raw power of natural elements—may be learned nowhere as forcefully as aboard a sailing ship.

The *Staatsraad Lemkuhl* is one of the three school ships operated by Norway. The young cadets will someday carry on the great seagoing traditions of their country. Aboard the sail ships they learn the real meaning of their future responsibilities by *doing* . . . and they do the work of men.

PHOTOS BY MICHAEL CHASSID

Mizzen brace haul aboard the *Staatsraad Lemkuhl* builds muscle and cooperative spirit as the ship heads for the open sea.

The young cadets learn quickly to climb the ratlines with confidence . . .

Looking aft as a brisk breeze comes up and the young cadets move out on the yard to unfurl the sails.

The sail begins to fill and the ship relies more and more on wind-power instead of her auxiliary engines.

. . and to work aloft as sure-footed and efficient as
d hands.

A single footrope is the margin between safety and a plunge to the deck
or the sea below.

on the yard arm the work is hard
risky.

The clew of a sail is carefully secured by a cadet.

Following the rule of the
old sailors: "One hand for
yourself, and one for the
ship."

Working aloft, making fast a block-and-tackle, coiling a line and stowing away gear properly—the routine skills demanded of sailors on sailing ships or steamers—are learned under the watchful eyes of the ship's officers. Many of the instructors began their sea careers as cadets on sail school ships. The youngsters in their charge receive personal attention and, sometimes, a helping hand.

A cadet kneads dough for baking bread . . .

. . . another youngster takes the wheel.

197

With the chart before him, the mate of the *Staatsraad Lemkuhl* checks the ship's course. Proud of the maritime traditions of their country, the officers aboard the sailing ships accept less than the average wages in the Merchant Marine.

Early morning duties for cadets include washing down the decks.

The future officers learn to peel potatoes as well as navigation.

Old rope is unlaid in the sail locker, the yarns to be used later as "baggy wrinkle" aloft to keep the stays from chafing against canvas.

Far from home, but happy nonetheless, a young sailor sits on the hatch and plays a tune for his shipmates.

Afterword

. . . vivid in our memory the beauty of the ships and the courage of the men who sailed them.

There are, in various parts of the United States, maritime museums which do a great deal to keep alive the nation's deepwater past. In other institutions, departments and special exhibits are devoted to different eras and aspects of maritime history. Some of the principal institutions are mentioned here. Others, not included for several technical reasons, nevertheless contribute importantly to the total effort.

The Marine Historical Association of Mystic, Connecticut, which has created Mystic Seaport, is outstanding. There is no similar institution which offers so much in so many fields of endeavor. In Mystic Seaport seagoing traditions are cherished and preserved; at the same time, through research, instruction, and active participation, the old is related to present-day life.

The Seaport, built on the winding, tidal Mystic River, is in all physical aspects a nineteenth century village with a cobbled quayside street. Houses typical of the period and of a seaport village are found along the street, and there are shops, a tavern, a counting-house, a ship-chandlery, a sail loft, a cooperage, a rope-walk where one may still see the old ways of making rope, and a blacksmith shop exactly as it might have been worked a hundred years ago.

Charles W. Morgan shoves her bowsprit towards the cobbles. She is the last of the New England wooden whaling ships. Next to her is the schooner *Bowdoin* which made twenty-six voyages to the Arctic; and then the slender, handsome full-rigger *Joseph Conrad* which Captain Alan Villiers sailed around the world; it had been built in 1882 in Copenhagen and was originally named *Georg Stage*.

Mystic Seaport on the river where many famous sailing ships were launched. The whaler *Charles W. Morgan* is moored alongside the main street of Mystic at the left. To the right is the *Joseph Conrad* which Alan Villiers sailed around the world.

The bow of the *Joseph Conrad* carries the likeness of the writer as its figurehead.

The ship's graceful lines can be seen in the construction of the stern.

The wheel and the steering compass aboard the *Joseph Conrad*.

The cabin skylight is made of teakwood. Beyond it is the fife rail where the gear hangs in neat fashion.

Mystic Seaport is much more than old buildings and ships. It has a fine planetarium where courses in celestial navigation are given. There is a large and modern library; exhibition halls hold thousands of carefully displayed objects.

Youngsters interested in the sea can qualify for several unusual courses.

Some of them live aboard the *Joseph Conrad* and stand watches during their stay. They are on the river in the daytime in a flotilla of dinghies, learning the first intricacies of sail handling. Others make a schooner cruise to Long Island Sound ports and the Port of New York, come back with hands and muscles hardened, and lasting memories. The past lives at Mystic.

Another remarkable institution is the Mariners Museum in Newport News, Virginia. Set in a magnificent sweep of lawn and forested park overlooking the James River, the museum possesses one of the finest maritime collections anywhere in the nation. From its inception, the Mariners Museum has been "devoted to the culture of the sea and its tributaries—its conquest by Man and its influence on Civilization." The exhibits are excellently arranged and rich in scope and variety. The lighting is superior to that of most other museums. The library is extraordinary both for the quality and number of its books on maritime subjects, and for its thousands of catalogued photographs.

Also outstanding is the museum on Nantucket Island, Massachusetts. Its exhibits and displays vividly recall the seagoing past; and the same is true for the museum at

The *Joseph Conrad* under sail at sea. She was formerly the *Georg Stag*, built in 1881-2 at Copenhagen. Today she represents as much as any vessel the finest traditions of the sailing ship.

Edgartown, Martha's Vineyard, Massachusetts; and the New Bedford, Massachusetts Whaling Museum, where half a whaling ship has been reconstructed and lies with her boats swung out.

The Peabody Museum at Salem, Massachusetts is the oldest in the country. It was founded in the eighteenth century by the shipmasters and supercargoes who sailed from the famous little port. Today its exhibits abound with details that bring back the drama of early America's commerce with China, India and the Spice Islands. Only part of the vast exhibit area is given over to maritime lore at the Division of Transportation, Smithsonian Institution, United States National Museum, in Washington, D.C. Yet so much is presented in carefully organized exhibits that a visit to this Museum becomes an exciting experience.

Sag Harbor, New York, where the nineteenth century whalers tacked home from Long Island Sound, has a fine museum that tells a great deal of maritime history. In fact, there are several in New York City, among them the Museum of the Seamen's Church Institute and the Museum of the Seamen's Bank for Savings.

New museums and maritime displays are also in preparation around the country. The National Maritime Historical Society at Washington, D.C., has plans to bring from the Philippines the last American-built clipper ship, *Kaiulani,* and install her in fully repaired condition in a Potomac River berth. The San Francisco Maritime Museum, which owns the square-rigger *Balclutha,* is expanding. The Maritime Museum Association of San Diego, California, is undertaking to do careful and extensive repair work on the square-rigged *Star of India.* A group of sea-minded, and public-spirited, citizens are working to save the schooner *Wawano* and keep her on display in a waterfront berth at Seattle, Washington.

The museums, the sailing enthusiasts of today and many devoted individuals merge into something of a national movement: together they preserve the sea traditions and keep vivid in our memory the beauty of the ships and the courage of the men who sailed them.

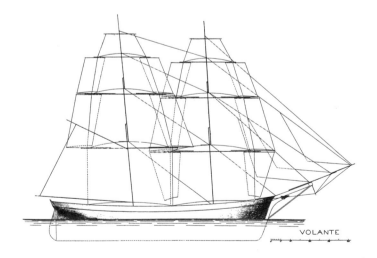

VOLANTE

Picture Credits

THE MARINERS MUSEUM, NEWPORT NEWS, VIRGINIA:
Senator (R. L. Hague Collection), p. 20; Deck scene, p. 21; *Flying Cloud* advertisement, p. 27; *Mount Stewart*, p. 33; *Roanoke*, p. 42; *Peter Rickmers* (Edwin Levick Collection), p. 43; *Wyoming* (Robert T. Little Collection), p. 44; *Lucy Evelyn* (William Abbe Collection), p. 46; *Whitebelle* (Edwin Levick Collection), p. 47; *Dalgonar* (Edwin Levick Collection), p. 52; *Arvan* (A. M. Barnes Collection), p. 54; *Preussen*, p. 54; *C. B. Pedersen* (Edwin Levick Collection), p. 55; *Everett C. Griggs* (Edwin Levick Collection), p. 57; *Falls of Halladale*, p. 58; *Belle O'Neill* (Edwin Levick Collection), p. 61; *Winterhude*, p. 61; *Vincent* (Edwin Levick Collection), p. 62 and 63; *Ben Vorlick*, p. 65; *Imperator Alexander* (Edwin Levick Collection), p. 67; Cape Horn engraving (Nautical Magazine), p. 68; Cape Horn (Edwin Levick Collection) p. 73; *Marjory Brown*, (Edwin Levick Collection), p. 87; *Brynhilda* (Edwin Levick Collection), p. 91; *Killeena* Levick Collection), p. 75; *Scotia* (A. M. Barnes Collection), p. 79; *Cromdale*, p. 79; *Maria Borges* (Robert T. Little Collection), p. 82–83; *Augustus Hunt* (H. B. Squires Collection), p. 84; *Ruth E. Merrill* (Robert T. Little Colection), p. 87; *Brynhilda* (Edwin Levick Collection), p. 91; *Killeena* (Edwin Levick Collection), p. 92; *Frank M. Deering* (Robert T. Little Collection), p. 94–95; *General Grant*, p. 95; *Annie G. Ross* (C. N. Rogers Collection), pp. 96–99; *Mariposa* (R. L. Hague Collection), p. 103; *Margaret L. Vinnen* (Edwin Levick Collection), p. 103; *Deerhill*, p. 104; Williamsburg Bridge and schooner (Edwin Levick Collection), p. 111; *Lizzie J. Cox* (M. V. Brewington Collection), p. 118; Fishing schooners, Boston (Robert T. Little Collection), p. 119; *Nova Queen* (Edwin Levick Collection), p. 132; *E. Starr Jones* (Edwin Levick Collection), p. 133; *Thomas W. Lawson*, pp. 123 and 124; Shipping at the pier, p. 136; *Rochambeau* (Edwin Levick Collection), p. 138–139; *Finland* (Edwin Levick Collection), p. 140; *M. Vivian Pierce* (Edwin Levick Collection), p. 143; Alaska packet fleet, p. 143; *Olivebank* (R. L. Hague Collection), p. 146; *Viking* (R. L. Hague Collection), p. 148–149; *Manunui* (Edwin Levick Collection), p. 156; *Governor Goodwin* (Mrs. C. W. Whidden), p. 158; *Bohemia* (Edwin Levick Collection), p. 159; *Laura* (Edwin Levick Collection), p. 160; *Ben Venue*, p. 165; Crew ready to go ashore (Eldredge Collection), p. 166; *John Ena*, et al. (Capt. J. Johnson, U.S.A., Ret.), p. 169; *Bangor* and *Caroline* (Capt. J. Johnson, U.S.A., Ret.), p. 170; *Abner Coburn* (Mark W. Hennessy), p. 170; *Fairhaven* (A. M. Barnes Collection), p. 170; *Morning Star*, p. 171; *Rights of Man*, p. 172; *Indiana* (Edwin Levick Collection), p. 172; *Carnegie* (Edwin Levick Collection, p. 173; *Jacob A. Stambler* (Edwin Levick Collection), p. 173; *Joseph Conrad*, p. 199–201.

THE SEAMEN'S BANK FOR SAVINGS, NEW YORK:
The Great Admiral, cover; *Red Jacket*, frontispiece; *Kirkcudbrightshire*, p. 16; Yankee clipper in Caribbean port, p. 18; *Great Western*, p. 19; East River, p. 19; Whampoa Harbor, p. 23; *Flying Cloud* model, p. 26; *Alabama*, p. 37; *Rainbow*, p. 70; *Tiger*, p. 70; *Young America*, p. 71; *Atlantic*, p. 106; *Western Metropolis*, p. 107; South Street, p. 108; East River, 1900, p. 109; New York Harbor, p. 110; *Columbia*, p. 121; *Thomas W. Lawson*, p. 124; *Shakespeare*, 184.

THE PEABODY MUSEUM OF SALEM, SALEM, MASSACHUSETTS:
Topsail schooner, p. 23; *Shannon*, p. 36; *Edward B. Winslow*, p. 40; *Baker Palmer*, pp. 48–51; *Alice*, p. 76; *Leona* and *Marion*, (E. S. Clark Collection), p. 79; Life Saving, p. 84; *Dora A. Baker*, p. 85; *Rhode Island*, p. 114; *Thomas W. Lawson*, p. 122–125; *Lucia A. Simpson*, p. 128; *Oliver Mitchell*, p. 129; *Rob Roy*, p. 142; *Governor Ames; Lizzie Brewster*, p. 144; *Katie D. Seavey* (E. S. Clark Collection), p. 145; *Cap Nord*, p. 153; *Laima*, p. 166; *Cora Cressy*, pp. 174–75.

THE SMITHSONIAN INSTITUTION, WASHINGTON, D.C.:
Savannah, p. 35; *Kite*, p. 38; *Wyoming*, p. 44; *Governor Ames*, p. 81; *Annie G. Ross*, p. 98; *Arthur James*, p. 116; *Harry Belden*, p. 117; *Leona M. Thurlow*, p. 120; *Alice M. Lawrence*, p. 134; *E. S. Newman*, p. 143.

FINNISH NATIONAL TRAVEL OFFICE, NEW YORK:
Olivebank, p. 146; *Penang*, p. 151; *Lawhill*, p. 152; Harbor of Mariehamn, p. 154–55; *Herzogin Cecilie*, p. 161; *Grace Harvar*, p. 163; *Passat*, p. 163; *Moshulu*, p. 168.

NORWEGIAN INFORMATION SERVICE, NEW YORK:
Sorlandet, p. 17; *Christian Radich*, p. 187.

DANISH INFORMATION OFFICE, NEW YORK:
Danmark, p. 190.

BRITISH INFORMATION SERVICE, NEW YORK:
Tawau, p. 190.

GERMAN INFORMATION CENTER:
Gorch Fock II, p. 188–189.

MYSTIC SEAPORT, MYSTIC, CONNECTICUT:
House at the Seaport, p. 28; Dining Room, p. 29; Living Room, p. 29; Ship's Galley, p. 31; Officers' Saloon, p. 31; *Charles W. Morgan* and *Joseph Conrad*, p. 199.

MICHAEL CHASSID:
Great Eastern, p. 102; *Lemkuhl* and Verrazano Bridge, p. 179; *Rotterdam* and *Radich*, p. 177; *Statsraad Lemkuhl*, Special Section, p. 193–199.

JEFF BLINN:
Sagres, p. 178; *St. Lawrence* and *Danmark*, p. 180–181; *Libertad*, p. 180; *Juan Sebastian de Elcano*, 181; *Esmeralda*, p. 184; *Eagle*, p. 186; *Dewarutji*, p. 191; *Sorlandet*, p. 191.

UNITED FRUIT COMPANY:
Jesse H. Freeman, p. 88; *Lorenzo Dow Baker*, p. 89; *Admiral Dewey*, p. 89.

CULVER PICTURES, INC.:
Empty ships, p. 22.

LAKE CARRIER'S ASSOCIATION:
Columbia, p. 127; *V. H. Ketchum*, p. 131.

WOODY GELMAN COLLECTION:
Clipper advertising cards, p. 71.

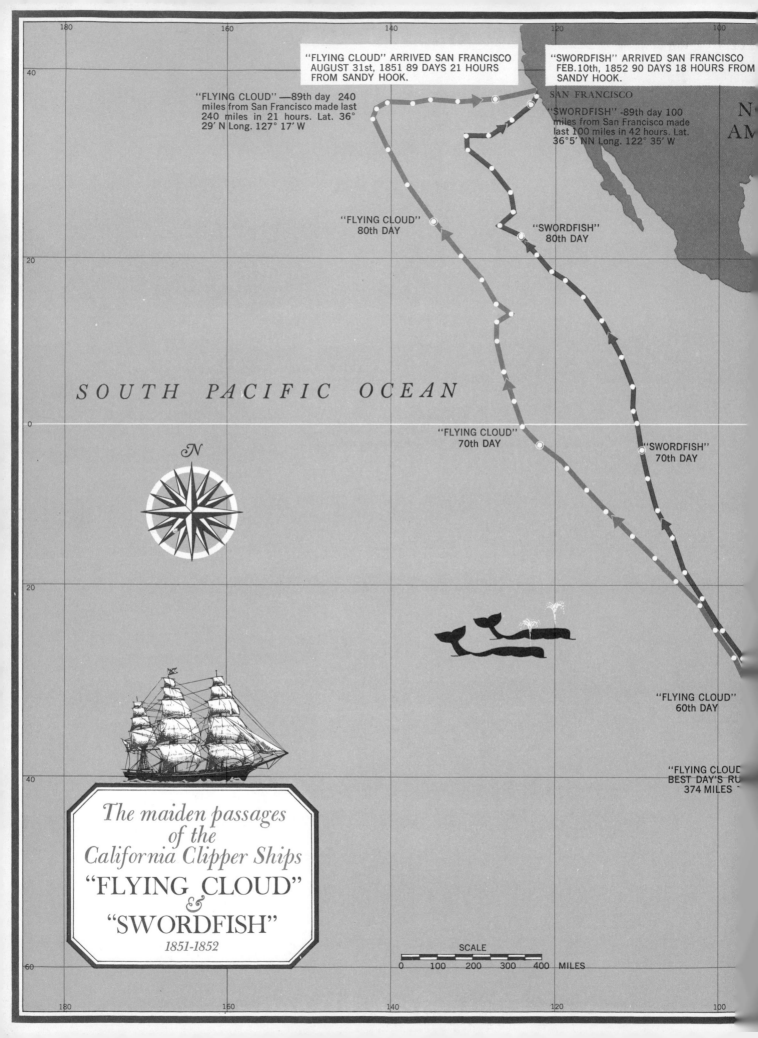